Zipporah, Queen of the Desert

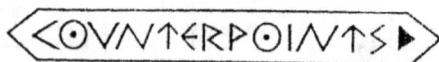
COUNTERPOINTS

Studies in Criticality

Shirley R. Steinberg
Series Editor

Vol. 553

Shoshana Rosenberg

Zipporah, Queen of the Desert

Living as Queer and Trans Jews in Australia

PETER LANG

New York · Berlin · Bruxelles · Chennai · Lausanne · Oxford

Library of Congress Cataloging-in-Publication Data

Names: Rosenberg, Shoshana, author.
Title: Zipporah, queen of the desert : living as queer and trans Jews in
Australia / Shoshana Rosenberg.
Description: New York : Peter Lang, 2024. | Series: Counterpoints,
1058-1634 ; vol. 553 | Includes bibliographical references and index.
Identifiers: LCCN 2024015295 (print) | LCCN 2024015296 (ebook) |
ISBN 9781636676401 (paperback) | ISBN 9781636676418 (pdf) |
ISBN 9781636676425 (epub)
Subjects: LCSH: Jewish gay people—Australia. | Jewish transgender
people—Australia.
Classification: LCC HQ76.3.A8 R67 2024 (print) | LCC HQ76.3.A8 (ebook) |
DDC 306.76/6089924094—dc23/eng/20240521
LC record available at https://lccn.loc.gov/2024015295
LC ebook record available at https://lccn.loc.gov/2024015296
DOI 10.3726/b21904

Bibliographic information published by the Deutsche Nationalbibliothek.
The German National Library lists this publication in the German
National Bibliography; detailed bibliographic data is available
on the Internet at http://dnb.d-nb.de.

Cover design by Peter Lang Group AG

ISSN 1058-1634 (print)
ISBN 9781636676401 (paperback)
ISBN 9781636676418 (ebook)
ISBN 9781636676425 (epub)
DOI 10.3726/b21904

Dedication
To radical Jewish queers, the Resistance, and all those fighting for a free Palestine and a free world.

TABLE OF CONTENTS

ACKNOWLEDGEMENTS

I would first like to acknowledge, pay tribute to, and express my ongoing solidarity with the peoples whose lands I was born and raised on. This includes the Palestinian people, the Whadjuk Noongar people, and the Wurundjeri people of the Kulin Nations. Their ongoing care and defence of their lands, at horrible and unimaginable costs both personal and collective, is something I kept and continue to keep at the front of my mind as I wrote this manuscript. I was privileged to be born amongst olive trees older than the nation-state that engulfed them, and just as privileged to grow up on lands and waters that have been fiercely protected in the face of colonization, genocide, and mass destruction.

I would also like to thank my mentor and friend Damien Riggs, without whom I would not have accomplished this seemingly impossible feat. Any person who has someone like him in their life should consider that life a blessed one.

Finally, I want to thank the people who have kept me afloat throughout the process of writing this book: my girlfriend Kate Pern, choreboy, Sophie Keeffe, Nic Menser Hearn, Dr. Nida Mollison, Cher Tan, Lyla Shlon, and Dan Thorpe.

INTRODUCTION

This book is the culmination of half a decade of research, interviews, and immersion in the internal, relational, and sociopolitical lives of queer Jewish people living in so-called Australia. It began as an extension of my research work into queer and trans peoples' experiences of sexuality, gender, relationships, and health, which I melded with my ongoing interest in Jewish culture, community, and spirituality. As part of this research I spoke with 17 queer and trans Jews from across so-called Australia about their experiences as Jews living in the Australian colony. I was incredibly fortunate to interview Jews of Colour, Jews who had moved states or countries in part due to their queerness, older Jews, younger Jews, Orthodox Jews, and atheist Jews. I spoke to queer and trans Jews who had left religious communities, left LGBT+ communities, found G-d, or felt like G-d needed to be left alone. I spoke with people who lived in queer and Jewish hubs, and people who lived in one shul towns (just about). Rather than trying to create a singular image from this wide range of experiences, I have chosen to let interviewees' words speak for them and to respond to them in the ways I felt most appropriate.

In this book you will find discussions of failure and growth, community abandonment and formation, relationships to Jewish traditions and culture, and history and contemporary life which have been thoroughly queered. These discussions were only as deep, meaningful, and honest as they were due to my shared experiences with those I interviewed. Therefore, before I begin this book in earnest, it is also important that the reader gets some understanding of how I am situated, and how I situate myself, in the world. I'm not interested in providing a chronological history or some kind of expanded biography. Instead I find myself compelled to explain things in metaphors or analogies or (most often) jokes, to revel in ambiguity, to hint at the multitudinous and densely layered nature of experience rather than try to concretely assert this or that aspect of my life. This book is about intersecting experiences, just like it says on the box. But in the same way you might proverbially[1] ask two Jews and get three opinions, a convergence of experiences produces excess, rather than an algebraic outcome. And so it is with this book as a whole, especially my lived experiences.

The "I" in Academia

This book is the result of a nearly five-year-long Doctoral process. Perhaps a pertinent thing to address right off the bat then is the use of first-person language throughout this Very Serious and Important Academic Product™. Here, already, there is excess. In the Neo-Liberal academic landscape I find myself in, Doctoral theses have been reduced to yet another milestone which increases your employability. Your thesis is a marker of your capacity to conduct and publish research in your field, but more importantly, its completion shows that you can produce viable work while employed at a full-time job that pays $14/hour. It is a flagellation, but I am not a Flagellant. It can feel undignified to talk about money, especially in an academic context where I am either seen as biting the hand that feeds or, worse, as someone who is exaggerating the truth of their circumstances. So for the sake of transparency, here are some of the other jobs (paid and unpaid) I held during my time as a Doctoral student:

- Lecturer,
- Tutor,
- Consultant,
- Research officer,
- Evaluation officer,
- Academic writer,
- Non-academic writer,

1 And often literally.

- Associate editor,
- Musician, and
- Leather maker.

This list is not exhaustive; it does not include all the labour required to keep me alive, safe, and as well as I can be. We will get to that later. So what does this have to do with the "I" in this book? Well firstly, to be blunt, this is *my* book. I do not believe in a kind of gun-toting, segregationist model of ownership so favoured by colonizers and oppressors, but I do believe that the Academy and its residents tend to forget who all this knowledge production belongs to. My work, and the work of other queer, trans, Jewish, and/or otherwise marginalized folk, does not belong to the Academy. It is not meant to be a singular hardcover gathering dust in a supervisor's office, or a collection of pay-walled articles only accessible to a privileged few. This "I" is more than it seems: it is not simply a matter of inserting myself into the Academy, of sticking my ugly little flag in its well-manicured lawn. The way "I" exists and persists, both in the realm of knowledge production and outside it[2], returns us to this matter of excess. It would be a radical oversimplification to view my existence as a multiply-marginalized person in several exclusionary spaces as just a matter of what I have previously described as "nominal visibility" [1]. That is to say, it is often the inclination of those who actively seek to defuse radical or contradictory voices in their field (and those who don't know any better) to reduce the presence of societal Others in these spaces to a mere matter of counting, of keeping any notion of diversity or progress restricted to what is materially present. The "I" scattered throughout the writing in this book becomes flattened through this lens, seen as a statement of personal perseverance and resilience or, perhaps more likely, a triumph on the part of my employers and publishers for supporting diversity amongst their ranks[3]. This book-long conversation between myself and the Academy does not produce some kind of accord, a marriage between my capacity to rise to the challenge of the pursuit of knowledge and the Academy's progressive inclusion policies and strategies. It produces *much more*, and perhaps not what you think.

We are deep in bitten feeding-hand territory here. I am not as grateful as I should be, even as I am personally given access to an incredible slew of resources, a meagre but liveable income, and arguably some kind of social

---

2 Though I and many others would argue that everything we do is knowledge production.

3 I make this statement from a place of both structural critique and lived experience, as is the case with most of the analysis in the work presented here and elsewhere.

capital[4]. That is because in this context, "I" represents much more than a number on a university's payroll, whether I like it or not. "I" am the product of a dense milieu of chance, a modicum of privilege, mentorship experiences ranging from tearjerkingly formative to negatively exemplary, and years of exhaustion-inducing and often degrading labour both within and outside the Academy. At a personal level, I find the flattening of this narrative either into some kind of individual queer/Jewish success story or, increasingly, the story of just another gay Jew working in academia, to be a significant disservice to myself and to those who have helped me get here.

More importantly, though, is the deep resonance I feel with Stephen Jay Gould's assessment of the myth of individual genius: "I am, somehow, less interested in the weight and convolutions of Einstein's brain than in the near certainty that people of equal talent have lived and died in cotton fields and sweatshops"[2]. I, too, am much less interested in exalting my so-called "personal achievements" and would rather spend my time acknowledging and meaningfully showing gratitude to the peoples, places, and phenomena who have landed me in this position[5]. I am not going to produce a laundry list of those who deserve the credit given to me like someone diagnosed with a terminal case of Imposter Syndrome, though of course their names and ideas will be cited and acknowledged throughout the thesis. Instead, I would like to acknowledge that "I" stands where I am largely because I have been a privileged witness to experiences, secrets, writings, and art made by people who will never see the proverbial inside of a Doctoral programme, or perhaps even a university classroom. There is nothing I have or know that was not developed through sharing, vulnerability, collaboration, and mutuality – this is the difference between I and "I", between what I consider to be a truly personal experience or achievement and what I consider to be the manifestation of all of that collective effort. I use this spelling as a way to humble myself, to express gratitude, and to recognize that "I" have only arrived here because so many others couldn't.

4 I would argue this capital is more costly than beneficial at times, but I try to keep a balanced perspective nonetheless.
5 I'm intentionally avoiding saying I was "helped" as many of these people have not intentionally assisted me; instead I would say I was privileged enough to be in their company or to have been exposed to their work, not to mention that I would argue many of the things which have shaped me have come at a cost to someone else's time, effort, and perhaps peace of mind.

Colonization, Israel, and Survival

"I" also literally stands where I am as a result of the colonization of First Nations peoples, as well as the result of my own experiences of abuse, fear, rampant nationalism, and the need to physically and geographically escape from multiple hostile situations. I escaped from one stolen land to another, at once benefitting from the colonial violence enacted on Aboriginal peoples and their Countries while simultaneously jettisoning my entire life thousands of kilometres away at 13 in order to avoid being coerced into violently enacting another nation-state's colonial bulldozing project, or becoming its victim. Or both. Here I use the notion of colonization broadly: colonial oppression does not solely manifest in geographic displacement and physical or sexual violence against Indigenous peoples – it is also a rigid social framework enacted upon colonized peoples and their now-stolen Country which creates and perpetuates these actions [3]. This social framework, while ostensibly borne largely of White Europeans' enamourment with racially singular global dominance, carries a set of epistemologically and structurally violent social rules which maintain and marginalize the Other in myriad forms [4]. Colonial anti-Bla(c) kness[6] leaks out of its racial parameters: it vilifies not only Bla(c)k people and People of Colour but fat people [6], disabled people [7], mad[7] people [10], trans people [11], queers [12], sex workers [13], and Jews [14], amongst many others. These are all people with bodyminds, faiths, and means of survival which are in direct contrast to the dictates of European colonization. Belonging to a multitude of these groups carries a sort of cumulative impact [15], an overdose of micromorts [16] – a *macromort*. The effect of being Othered by colonial powers is not measured by grains of sand but by sacks.

This is of course not to say that people who exist within these intersections are not also capable of perpetuating settler-colonial mentalities and behaviours. Our choices are often limited. We inevitably regurgitate that which we have been forced to swallow whole, or else we die with it stuck in our throats. Or both. It is impossible to deny the vital role of homonationalism in softening the image of the settler-colonial atrocities in Israel [17], or the way white queer voices continue to dominate and drown out queer People of Colour [18, 19]. At the same time, it is also impossible to deny that homophobic and transphobic

---

6 This spelling influenced by Yadira Perez Hazel's [5] beautiful paper on the term's unification of the experiences of Black people in the US and Blak people in settler-colonial Australia.

7 For further reasoning on why I use this term, I recommend Ted Curtis' *Mad Pride* [8] or Mohammed Abouelleil Rashed's *Madness and the Demand for Recognition* [9].

violence shapes the lives of all involved parties, whether they are mimicking oppressive structures or not. This is not an absolution, but it is an explanation.

I am a product of colonization: my ancestors survived Pogroms, genocide, forced displacement, and perhaps the unkindest cut of all, an eventual geopolitical sequestering which positioned myself and two generations before me as Jewish people living on "Jewish" land, far far away from the countries who enabled our destruction en masse. But this was not a matter of Jewish safety – it was a matter of distance, control, and a poisoning of the well from which both Jewish settlers and Indigenous Palestinians drink. Holocaust survivors forced to flee to Palestine were fed a colonial narrative that went beyond intellect, manifesting in the body itself. The solution offered to millions of starving, traumatized Jews was not one of comfort but one of a fully embodied colonial mindset obsessed with strength, stoicism, and "might makes right" – what Todd Samuel Presner [20] described as *muscular Judaism*. The colonial story of Israel maintains that the nation-state was established by, and continues to thrive because of, the physical effort and intellectual sharpness of settlers [21] – an oasis in a desert, made entirely by our hands. In other words, the story of Israel is one which disregards Palestinians' particular approach to their land, developed over centuries, in favour of colonial understandings of thriving – build more, build higher, build further. Most importantly, *work harder*.

And while it is true that many early settlers built their houses, cities, schools, and hospitals from the ground up, this narrative of hard work conceals an important question: why were these our reparations? Our bodyminds were already shaped by colonial powers, emaciated and downtrodden[8] by centuries of isolation and periods of intensive ethnic cleansing. We were made unwelcome in our countries of birth, our communities, and our homes. The creation of Israel, then, seemed like a welcome reprieve, a shifting of the balance towards Jewish self-determination. But the reality is, we did not need to build new homes; those that were not burned down or occupied were still standing, awaiting our return. Instead, we continue to be cattle-prodded by the logic of "arbeit macht frei" ("work sets you free"), though Auschwitz is now long gone. We had to earn our homes in the Holy Land so that we could be free from the antisemitism still thriving elsewhere. Our liberation was a conditional one, with *many* clauses embedded in the fine print. We could have new homes, *but we mustn't ask what happened to our old ones*. We could have our own economy, *but we mustn't ask where the wealth from our ransacked homes and bodies had*

---

8 Often both literally and figuratively.

gone. We could have some notion of collective identity *but at the cost of our diverse cultures*. Perhaps most importantly, we could have safety, *we just had to work for it a little longer*. And a little longer. And a little longer.

The "new Jewish body" [20] was not formed by relief, comfort, or safety. Though we had been starved, we could not become fleshy. Though we had been weakened, we could not succumb to that weakness. Though we had been brought to the brink of annihilation, we could not grieve. We simply transitioned from one form of survival to another, from the desperation caused by raided shtetls and mass death to the desperation of a displaced, disparate group of people forced onto another's Indigenous land. Whether labouring in a concentration camp or labouring to dry up swamplands for new settlements [22], the running theme is still labour. I use present tense here because this is not historical: the mainstream political landscape of my birth country is one where resistance to this notion of constant work is seen as an extreme outlier, ironically often held up by Orthodox and otherwise Halakhically observant people [23]. Our imagination has been constricted by this perceived inevitability of perpetual work as the only solution to misery, to unkindness, to existential threat [24, 25]. Through this lens, hard work is not seen as something that yields reward but rather something that *keeps us alive*. This is the legacy of all those subjected to colonization, and one of the most assured ways out of this *perpetual cycle* [26] is through the decolonizing approaches which have been developed by Bla(c)k people and People of Colour over decades and centuries of oppression [27].

It's important that I state here that while I am using decolonizing frameworks as part of my practice, I am strictly opposed to any kind of post-hoc "self-Indigenization" [28]. I am not interested in intellectual or religious notions of nationalistic birthright. I am not Indigenous to occupied Palestinian territory. Indigeneity is a matter of deep, uninterrupted connection with, and custodianship of, a land and all its occupants [29]. This connection forms over centuries, millennia. My Jewish roots are deep, but they extend elsewhere. My roots have also been severed, sometimes recovered but often lost forever. It would be disingenuous to claim an ancestral connection to a land my grandmother and namesake arrived at when she was 12, alone on a boat illegally transporting survivors to the Palestinian mainland; a land which my family ran to only as a means of escape from a corrupt, violent, destructive nineteenth- and twentieth-century Europe. As Jonathan Boyarin [30] points out, if this is all to be accepted as fact, then we are forced to contend with the knowledge that the project of Israel is not a decolonial, liberatory tale; it is a story of desperation, displacement, and colonial machinations which deprive both Jews and Palestinians of sovereignty, safety, and peace.

Corpulent Judaism

When I saw Roxane Gay describe herself as "corpulent" [31], something clicked. If *muscular Judaism* represents an internalization and embodiment of colonial thinking, then what better form of refusal is there than *corpulence*? These logics are focused on the *musculus*, on those things that we can (mostly) control, develop, and use as a tool. My logic extends to the entire *corpus*, recognizing there are things we have a modicum of control over, but so many more that we do not. I cannot will my skin to heal quicker, or my organs to improve function. I cannot fully control how much pain I experience, or whether this or that foodstuff will be absorbed and processed correctly. Ironically, *muscular Judaism* as a framework contains no steadfast answers on how to deal with the whole body, precisely because you cannot "deal" with bodies in their entirety. Much of it is, and always will be, out of our control.

Here we return to this notion of excess. Muscularity opposes excess, toiling endlessly to strip away fat in a vain attempt at self-discipline. Corpulence, by contrast, is perhaps one of the most reviled forms of excess: it is viscerally felt, visible, and undeniably imbued with notions of laziness, of lack of contribution, of ill-health and its burden on the person and those around them [32]. To be corpulent is to fail, to waiver one's right to humanity on the basis of their perceived contribution. In case the reader has any doubt in their mind, I need to make it clear that *I* am corpulent. I describe my corpulence in a variety of ways: I'm a brick shithouse, a vault door, a person-and-a-half. These are hyperbole, but they are not pejorative, not to me, not anymore. Instead, they are markers of resistance. If it weren't for the way my body is, I would not be writing these words. If I was not informed early on that my body is an aberration, that my fatness demarcates me as lesser, that my size is a fundamental flaw of my existence, I would perhaps have been deprived of coming to terms with just how strange a bird I really am. Through a combination of genetics, heavy-duty life events, and medical negligence based on my excess-laden body, pain has also become a consistent aspect of my life.

Call it a Northern Star, call it a fast-moving meteor, but this excess of fat and misfiring nociceptors certainly forms a part how "I" earned a spot at a Doctoral programme. The Academy is deeply flawed and reflects many of the broader issues discussed in this chapter so far [33], but it is also one of the few areas of work where the demand for intense physical labour is distinctly reduced. Not to overextend an analogy, but there are days where I feel myself begrudge academia in the same way I begrudge my birthplace. I have worked towards academic excellence since childhood[9], not early partly because of my interests but also partly because intellectual work was just what was expected of such a corpulent person. Writing is what solitary people do, and there are few words to describe the majority of my life which encompass it quite as succinctly as "solitary".

As I got older, and my body bigger and more riddled with pain, my options became increasingly limited. Manual labour became out of the question[10], and my ever-present and ever-increasing size has made me a target of disdain and unnecessary violence in the majority of public-facing jobs[11]. My scope of options for employment, and more to the point survival, has been narrowing since childhood. So I found myself investing in what I (thought I) could control: my mind. This too would become a lifelong negotiation, riding the waves of psychosis and negotiating mental riptides which have erased weeks and months of my life. But compared to physical pain, mental anguish felt like a beast I could tame. I think this is the case of *no good choices* that many sick and mad people face; you are often forced to contain one form of disability or difference so that you do not have to negotiate another as intensely. I can't help but feel embittered by these non-options, even if I no longer make the majority of my money in ways that leave me in permanent physical agony. I am not here because of my desire to learn and grow but due to my desperate drive to survive in a world that does not see me as a valuable citizen.

This nexus of suffering is a point of convergence for masculinity, white supremacy, and neoliberal frameworks of existence. The types of work I have found myself in time and time again, even when I had more physiological capacity, have come under one denigrated category of labour or another. Working at a university has certainly provided many opportunities to experience internalized shame: it is "feminised" work (read: lesser, weaker) [34, 35], it is "Jewish" work (read: non-laborious, soft, stereotypical) [36, 37], and it is work that is

---

9 With a short several-years-long break between dropping out of high school and returning to university.

10 In fact, manual labour is part of the reason why I can't work doing manual labour.

11 You would perhaps be surprised to learn that working in crisis and mental health support services as a 6'4", very wide person radically dichotomizes people's responses to you; you are seen as either too much of threat to even attempt or as a goal to be conquered. And don't think for a second that this is any different at a bar or factory.

positioned as being in direct opposition to working class struggles [38, 39]. As someone existing and persisting within working class, Jewish womanhood, it is impossible to avoid regularly contending with (and being existentially irked by) these contradictory perspectives. The Venn diagram of women (and other people perceived as "feminine"), Jews, and the working class has more overlap than overhang [40, 41], but that fact is obscured by these intersecting points of masculinist and oppressive denigration and divisiveness.

I would like to make one thing very clear: there is no form of work that is purely intellectual or purely physical, nor is there work that is unequivocally good or bad[12]. I could protest and state that academic work requires strength, that it is highly laborious and all-consuming, that the Academy also relies on employees who are rigidly kept within the lower/working classes and are increasingly existing within what Chris Dunkley has described as the *Precariat* [42]. But my point is not that all people experience work in the same way, nor that academics are somehow the truly downtrodden group. I'm also not interested in rescuing the Academy's image so much as I am interested in cultivating an understanding of societal contribution and collective action that moves beyond the scope of physical capacity as the main determinant of human value. My work and my life are of value even if I am not working myself to physical exhaustion; conversely, the lives of those who do physical labour to survive have value far beyond what their bodies can endure. I am divesting from finding value only through the brutal exploitation of our bodies and the debasement of dialogic and collective knowledge production, and I hope you are doing the same.

Within the context of this manuscript, these considerations underpin this concept of *corpulent Judaism*: a type of Jewishness that embraces and valorizes excess, strangeness, difference, pleasure, and, perhaps most importantly, *rest* [43]. It is a Jewishness that enthusiastically accepts its place amongst the many spectres which haunt the settler-colonial state, rather than rejecting the mantle as a means of safety-via-assimilation [44]. This is not a new kind of Judaism but more of a political counterpoint to the endless, centuries-old yoke of Jews having to earn our safety in every society we live in. This drive to perpetual work as the key to survival not only created a massive Jewish slave underclass who were often forced to abandon their faith and communities but also a small group of wealthier and undoubtedly more assimilated Jews who re-enacted their own ancestral oppression by owning both Jewish and non-Jewish slaves

---

12 We can discuss people working to maintain the Prison Industrial Complex at another point in time.

[45]. This division epitomizes *muscular* Jewish ideology. You are either owned or you are an owner; you are either the "right" kind of Jew or you are the "wrong" kind; you are either a productive citizen or a burdensome bludger. This lineage tracks to the modern day, where the *muscular* Israeli state violently demarcates their upper class from lower classes along the same lines as our own oppressors [46].

If this is what *muscle* looks like, then I am far more interested in *fat*. *Muscle* is tightly wound; *fat* expands, pressing endlessly against the skin, always moving towards the horizon. *Muscle* thrives on discipline and rigidity; *fat* thrives on pleasure, softness, comfort, and rest. *Muscle* looks like Ori Hofmekler telling you, a "warrior", how long you need to starve each day in order to have a "leaner, harder body" [47]; *fat* looks like Susan Bordo and her sisters co-writing a whole chapter about the complex interplay and beauty of food, kitchens, families, and bodies [48]. *Muscle* claims that survival is only achieved by strength and control; *fat* knows there is already enough for us all to feast on, and that survival is a poor replacement for collective opulence. *Muscle* rules by the sword; *fat* needs no ruler to thrive.

Living and Researching with Complexity

Our current environment of knowledge production requires that I take all of these insights, all the diverse and complex experiences I have described so far, and funnel them down into a digestible outcome. The complete Doctoral manuscript, so I'm told, is intended to neatly encapsulate everything into איפה הייתי ומה עשיתי (*ei'fo ha'iti ve'ma a'siti*, translation: *where did I go and what did I do*). I need to tell you where I started, where I'd gone, and what I did when I got there. In case the original sentence does not fully betray this, it is the equivalent of show and tell. To act as if this project began when I enrolled, or that it will be done when I complete my contracted number of words on a page, is to disregard how intertwined all of these processes are. Every conversation, accident, artwork, or fuck I've experienced has the potential to tick the fundamental boxes of research: I go through a new (or even old or repeating) experience → I internalize and contemplate this experience → I use this experience to guide my future thoughts and actions → I share my insights with others, which often leads me immediately back to the start of the loop. The following chapters will further unpack the reductivism which rules the academic roost and its impact on those of us who do not see things so linearly or with as much of an illusion of "objectivity". But in order to understand this excess, this *corpulence,* it felt important to begin this manuscript with a stripping bare of the fundamental issues which leak, overlap, and mess up the categories which so rigidly define what a doctoral process is supposed to look like, what my life is supposed to look like, and how the interaction between the two is supposed to look like. Here's to defying expectations, either by exceeding them or by choosing instead to fail.

References

[1] Sharp M, Rosenberg S. *Technoqueering and Music: The Use of Sound, Gender and Technology.* Springer, 2021.

[2] Gould SJ. *The Panda's Thumb: More Reflections in Natural History.* W. W. Norton & Company, 2010.

[3] Behrendt L. *Achieving Social Justice: Indigenous Rights and Australia's Future.* Federation Press, 2003.

[4] Chan D, Farquhar M, Garbutt R, et al. A case for reimagining Australia: Dialogic registers of the Other, truth-telling and a will to justice. *Coolabah* 2018; 0: 199–212.

[5] Yadira Perez Hazel P. Bla(c)k Lives Matter in Australia. *Transition* 2018; 59–67.

[6] Strings S. *Fearing the Black Body: The Racial Origins of Fat Phobia.* NYU Press, 2019.

[7] Grech S. Decolonising eurocentric disability studies: Why colonialism matters in the disability and global South debate. *Soc Identities* 2015; 21: 6–21.

[8] Dellar R, Curtis T, & Esther L. *Mad Pride.* Chipmunkapublishing ltd, 2011.

[9] Rashed MA. *Madness and the Demand for Recognition: A Philosophical Inquiry into Identity and Mental Health Activism.* Oxford University Press, 2019.

[10] Hickling FW. Owning our madness: Contributions of Jamaican psychiatry to decolonizing Global Mental Health. *Transcult Psychiatry* 2020; 57: 19–31.

[11] Boellstorff T, Cabral M, Cárdenas M, et al. Decolonizing transgender: A roundtable discussion. *TSQ Transgender Stud Q* 2014; 1: 419–439.

[12] Smith A. Queer theory and native studies: The heteronormativity of settler colonialism. *GLQ J Lesbian Gay Stud* 2010; 16: 41–68.

[13] Boonzaier F. Researching sex work: Doing decolonial, intersectional narrative analysis. In Boonzaier, F., Fleetwood, J., Presser, L., Sandberg, S. and Ugelvik, T. (eds.), Emerald Handbook of Narrative Criminology, Bingley UK Emerald, pp. 467–491.

[14] Davis C. *Colonialism, Antisemitism, and Germans of Jewish Descent in Imperial Germany.* University of Michigan Press, 2012.

[15] Constance-Huggins M, Mwangi EW, Gibson A. Women of C ‡ref_titleBook olor: Using Intersectionality Theory to Explore Cumulative Disadvantages in Health Outcomes. *SEWSA 2016 Intersect New Millenn Assess Cult Power Soc,* <https://digitalcommons.winth rop.edu/sewsa/2016/fullschedule/89> (2016).

[16] Fry AM, Harrison A, Daigneault M. Micromorts – what is the risk? *Br J Oral Maxillofac Surg* 2016; 54: 230–231.

[17] Puar JK. Homonationalism as assemblage: Viral travels, affective sexualities. *Jindal Glob Law Rev* 2013; 4: 23–43.

[18] Rault J. White noise, white affects: filtering the sameness of queer suffering. *Fem Media Stud* 2017; 17: 585–599.

[19] Petzen J. Queer Trouble: Centring Race in Queer and Feminist Politics. *J Intercult Stud* 2012; 33: 289–302.

[20] Presner TS. *Muscular Judaism: The Jewish Body and the Politics of Regeneration.* Routledge, 2007.

[21] Boyarin D. *The No-State Solution: A Jewish Manifesto.* Yale University Press, 2023.

[22] Marom R. A short history of Mulabbis (Petah Tikva, Israel). *Palest Explor Q* 2019; 151: 134–145.

[23] Stadler N. Is profane work an obstacle to salvation? The case of ultra orthodox (Haredi) Jews in contemporary Israel. *Sociol Relig* 2002; 63: 455–474.

[24] Fisher M. *Capitalist Realism: Is There No Alternative?* John Hunt Publishing, 2009.

[25] Goode L, Godhe M. Beyond capitalist realism: Why we need critical future studies. *Cult Unbound* 2017; 9: 108–129.

[26] Assück. Perpetual Cycle. Sound Pollution Records, <https://gen ius.com/Ass uck-perpet ual-cycle-lyrics> (1991, accessed 10 November 2020).

[27] Ng WWW. *Racing Solidarity, Remaking Labour: Labour Renewal from a Decolonizing and Anti-racism Perspective.* Thesis, <https://tsp ace.libr ary.utoro nto.ca/han dle/1807/26495> (2011, accessed 10 November 2020).

[28] Pearson S. "The Last Bastion of Colonialism": Appalachian settler colonialism and self-indigenization. *Am Indian Cult Res J* 2013; 37: 165–184.

[29] Sarivaara E, Maatta K, Uusiautti S. Who is indigenous? Definitions of indigeneity. *Eur Sci J* 2013; 369–378.

[30] Boyarin J. *Storm from Paradise: The Politics of Jewish Memory.* U of Minnesota Press, 1992.

[31] Gay R. *Hunger: A Memoir of (My) Body.* Hachette UK, 2017.

[32] Bordo S. *Unbearable Weight: Feminism, Western Culture, and the Body.* University of California Press, 2004.

[33] Lourens H. Supercripping the academy: The difference narrative of a disabled academic. *Disabil Soc* 2020; 0: 1–16.

[34] Parker I. Psychotherapy under capitalism: The production, circulation and management of value and subjectivity. *Psychother Polit Int* 2014; 12: 166–175.

[35] Craig ML, Liberti R. "'Cause That's What Girls Do": The making of a feminized gym. *Gend Soc* 2007; 21: 676–699.

[36] Boyarin D, Itzkovitz D, Pellegrini A. Strange bedfellows: An introduction. *Queer Theory and the Jewish Question* 2003; 1–18.

[37] Hollinger DA. *Science, Jews, and Secular Culture: Studies in Mid-twentieth-Century American Intellectual History.* Princeton University Press, 1998.

[38] Negraeff LE 1982–. *The Whole Is in Every Part: A Working-Class Woman's Experiences in Academia.* Thesis, University of Saskatchewan, <https://harv est.usask.ca/han dle/10388/10961> (2018, accessed 24 November 2020).

[39] Rickett B, Morris A. "Mopping up tears in the academy" – working-class academics, belonging, and the necessity for emotional labour in UK academia. *Discourse Stud Cult Polit Educ* 2020; 0: 1–15.

[40] Boos F. *Memoirs of Victorian Working-Class Women: The Hard Way Up*. Palgrave Macmillan. Epub ahead of print 2017. DOI: 10.1007/978-3-319-64215-4.

[41] Balthaser B. When anti-Zionism was Jewish: Jewish racial subjectivity and the anti-Imperialist Literary Left from the Great Depression to the Cold War. *Am Q* 2020; 72: 449–470.

[42] Dunkley C. *The Precariat*. Oberon Books, 2013.

[43] Hersey T. *Rest Is Resistance: A Manifesto*. Hachette UK, 2022.

[44] Medding P. *From Assimilation to Group Survival: A Political and Sociological Study of an Australian Jewish Community*. Cheshire, 1968.

[45] Hezser C. *Jewish Slavery in Antiquity*. OUP Oxford, 2005.

[46] Ghanem A ad. Israel's second-class citizens: Arabs in Israel and the struggle for equal rights. *Foreign Aff* 2016; 95: 37.

[47] Hofmekler O. *The Warrior Diet: Switch on Your Biological Powerhouse for High Energy, Explosive Strength, and a Leaner, Harder Body*. Blue Snake Books, 2007.

[48] Bordo S, Klein B, Silverman MK. Missing Kitchens. In: *Twilight Zones: The Hidden Life of Cultural Images from Plato to O.J.* University of California Press, 1999.

· 1 ·

SWIRLING TOWARDS FREEDOM: HERMENEUTICS, DECOLONIZING METHODOLOGIES, AND QUEER JEWISH APPROACHES TO QUALITATIVE RESEARCH

> Jewish culture, like any literary tradition based on canonical writings, is haunted by the problem of validating later developments against its earlier, authoritative formulations [1]

Jewishness exists in perpetual oscillation, torn between its core teachings which compel its adherents to question, dissect, and challenge current knowledges, and those which stratify Jewish life down to the (literal) letter [2–4]. In a sense, melding the two worldviews together is one of the greatest ongoing puzzles of Jewishness both as a communal and personal practice. One might feel the need to pick a side; to decide whether you prefer to view Judaism's teachings as a source for answers, or as a source for more questions [5].

Few cultural paradigm shifts have highlighted the conflict between doctrinal observance and scepticism quite as well as the increasing visibility of queerness in Judaism. While the thread of queer narratives in Judaism extends back centuries, arguably existing alongside and within the tradition for as long as there has been a tradition [6, 7], Judaism continues to have a complicated, often exclusionary, approach to queerness writ large. Religious doctrines, and their adherents, position queer people as deviants [8, 9], thereby condemning those who are aligned with it [10]. Meanwhile, even in secular Judaism-dominated communities and places, including Israel, Jewish queer people encounter resistance, rejection, and discrimination based on their experiences of sexuality and gender[1] [12–14]. While perceptions of, and engagement with, queerness is slowly shifting across the Jewish spectrum [15, 16], it remains a point of tension between queer Jews and their heterosexual and/or cisgender counterparts.

As a queer Jewish person, I have found myself at odds with the apparent monolith of Jewish rejection of queerness. As a result, I felt driven to dedicate my Doctorate to exploring the lived experiences of Jewish people in my corner of the world. There is little research on queer Jewish experiences in Australia, with even the most well-recruited national survey of Australian Jewish communities failing to include any questions on sexuality or gender [17]. I found it simultaneously disappointing and fascinating to notice such a disregard for two of the most core aspects of life, particularly considering Judaism's pleasure-based and often mystical perspective on sex and gender [18], not to mention our relationship with so-called social outcasts and revolutionary heretics [19]. There is a kind of self-inflicted epistemological violence at play, an othering-by-omission of something that appears to be a core aspect of our own culture and history [20, 21].

Methodologies

Jewish Methodologies

While pursuing phenomenological documentation and analysis of queer Jewish experiences has formed the major part of my Doctoral undertaking, I found myself equally fascinated with what radical perspectives (nominally queer or otherwise) can be taken into the research process itself. In particular, I sought to further explore how the hermeneutic principles which make up so much of the cyclical process of Jewish questioning mentioned at the beginning of this chapter can be applied radically and, most importantly, queerly in this context. Extending the notion that "we both transform and are transformed by texts" [22] to the structures of the research itself has become a queer Jewish pursuit in and of itself throughout this project.

Hermeneutics is core to how Jewish tradition and culture are structured and has been present in one form or another for centuries [23]. Simply put,

---

1 Although not all transgender, non-binary, or otherwise gender non-conforming people identify with queerness as a title [11], this chapter uses the term "queer" to imply any transgression from normative models of sexuality and gender.

hermeneutics is an approach to textual analysis which views the reader and the text as inseparable entities, whose interaction produces knowledge and meaning which can significantly transform both parties. Hermeneutics provides a contrast point to reductionist perceptions of knowledge and methods [24], instead offering a perspective that is always inquiring, and always evolving collective and personal comprehensions of the world around us. Elliot R. Wolfson [25] describes the pursuit of hermeneutics as a sacred duty, a process which has radical and mystical roots and manifestations. For them, the perpetual interpretative mechanism is a path all people, but Jews in particular, are encouraged to walk down. This idea had particular appeal to me as someone who has only begun to pray after beginning their PhD on Jewishness, this idea of trusting a path rather than making it. Additionally, I found Wolfson's [26] analysis of Gadamer's Truth and Method [27] incredibly useful and forceful. They suggest that one of the core challenges and benefits of hermeneutics is its consideration of interpreting a text while allowing others to be considered, to coexist. This is where queer thinking on the subject provides a bridge to hermeneutic considerations of gender and sexuality.

Queer Jewish Methodologies

Donald E. Hall's [28] work has significantly informed this particular study, as well as my research career in general. *Reading Sexualities*, Hall's most relevant work on the subject, forms a kind of meeting place, between the questioning and listening that is so core to both the use of hermeneutics broadly (and Jewish thought specifically), and the ways in which the presence of queerness (embodied or conceptual) disrupts and at times completely upturns oppressive or narrow social ethics and structures. Their writing suggests that treating sex, gender, and relationships as texts allows us to understand the ways in which our inner, relational, and communal selves affect and are affected by other "texts". While text as sex, and vice versa, has been explored for some time (e.g. [29]), Hall's positioning of queerness as a genuine transformative force moved me, and moves us, away from the aforementioned obsession with a reductionist "truth" and towards the ever-evolving nature of Truth.

In a more direct response to Wolfson's concern with acknowledging the co-existence of multiple narratives as part of the hermeneutic process, Eve Kosofky Sedgewick's [30] writing provides a second queer anchoring. In particular, Sedgewick's later writing explicates the ways queer narratives are not buried beneath oppressive histories, but rather exist *beside* them, awaiting to be attended to. This is not to say that Jewish queerness and radical sexual exploration have not been very literally buried or destroyed, especially considering events such as the Nazi burning of the Zeitschrift für Sexualwissenschaft, a Sexological institute which employed many Jewish academics [31], or the Nazi regime's doubled persecution of queer Jews [32–34]. Rather, it is an indication of the queer undercurrents in all societies which have resisted capture and succeeded in taking root, even in societies which openly treat people it deems as queer with hostility, persecution, incarceration, and death.

Perhaps the most controversial and yet vital thinking on how Jewishness and queerness intermix comes from Janet R. Jakobsen's essay *Queers Are Like Jews, Aren't They? Analogy and Alliance Politics* [35]. This essay examines the intertwining histories of queerness and Jewishness not as lived experiences but as conceptual frameworks which position Jews and queers as a collective Other. While this conflation was one of the main tools used to incite anti-Jewish and anti-queer sentiments and actions throughout European history, it also highlights the queer elements which form many traditional, cultural, and embodied aspects of Judaism and Jewish people. Jakobsen discusses some common narratives of queer/Jewish conflation, such as the "switched gender roles" which exemplify (heterosexual) Jewish relationships and the displacement of focus on the body and the physical in favour of the mind and the spiritual. Most importantly, they highlight the ways in which the idea of a Jew has historically had little distinction from the idea of a queer, particularly in terms of its implication of a person or peoples being soft, deviant, or otherwise unfit for the society they existed within. This reductive, singular perspective of Jewishness as "weakness" (read: queerness) has formed a part of some of the most violent regimes in the world. In its most extreme cases, under Nazi rule, this created what Boaz Noyman [36] described as a "פלנטה" (planet), an insular and self-contained bubble which drew and enforced distinct lines between the "living world" of the Nazis and the "dead world" which the Jews were forced to live in. It is perhaps this idea of an uninterrupted ideology-turned-genocide which stands as my longest-running motivation to engage in hermeneutics not only philosophically and academically but also as a part of practical solidarity work which is aimed at disrupting oppressive, divisive, and dehumanizing perceptions of any person or group.

Queer, Jewish, Decolonizing Methodologies

In this spirit, it has become abundantly clear that my work cannot be complete without considering the thinking and practices of other oppressed peoples.

Specifically, alongside the contributions of Jewish and queer thought to my methodological framework, I remain grateful for my exposure to First Nations narratives of survival, truth, and community-building throughout my academic and personal life. As Colin Tatz [37] suggests, there is first and foremost a moral imperative for Jewish people to engage with First Nations peoples and their experiences, as Jewish traditions and law dictate the need to be אור לגויים (a light to other nations / Or La'Goyim), to contribute meaningfully to improving others' lives wherever we reside. Jews have also been subject to many of the same structural and societal harms that First Nations peoples in Australia and elsewhere have experienced historically and continue to experience in the present day. But perhaps most importantly, while we do share these histories of suppression, more recent invocations of "the Jewish people" as a populace have been directly responsible for transgressions against First Nations peoples. This is most apparent in the ongoing oppression of Palestinians by the Israeli government, under the guise of Jewish settlers' supposed birthright and "disrupted indigeneity" to the land in question [38, 39]. It is therefore not only a duty for all researchers, Jewish or otherwise, to engage with Indigenous ways of thinking in the abstract spaces of philosophy and art but also to apply them in praxis and include First Nations peoples' voices and perspectives into our everyday processes.

Arguably the book that first properly propelled me into research was Shawn Wilson's *Research Is Ceremony* [40]. In a combination of early queerness and a barely dormant fascination with BDSM, I discovered the book through a piece of dialogue posted on a punk blog which referenced a First Nations supervisor suggesting to their First Nations student that if they would like to make their Masters graduation more spiritually connective and Indigenous, they should make a ritualized knife cut under one eye when they finish their Masters and another for their PhD. Something about this felt both intensely Jewish and queer, in its refusal to legitimize the academy while still legitimizing the need to find and clarify knowledge and knowledge-making. It was my first time reading a piece of theory work that was so focused on praxis while defying most of what I ever thought was right about academia. Wilson describes in detail their experiences working with First Nations communities, students, and academics; alongside interview data, Wilson provides an evolving framework of connection between research and reality. They explicate the need for researchers to connect to the land, to the other people, to yourself, and to the Universe. This is not posited as a suggestion but as a legitimate paradigm shift in research practices which is geared at yielding research that is more legitimate in its representation of, and benefit to, First Nations (and by extension other) peoples.

I saw much of my Jewish understanding of knowledge reflected in Wilson's writing, this connection between embodied living and the creation, learning, and archival of knowledge. For all the societal narratives of Jews as being unconcerned with their bodies, of prioritizing brains over brain, my experience of Jewishness overwhelmingly has been that of Jews as a people who have protected their knowledge with their literal physical bodies, sometimes to the point of death. These are the same feelings I have towards queerness, and the way our culture had to survive the AIDS epidemic, systematic homophobia and transphobia, and the phenomenal risk inherent in having to step out of the bounds of the law or Western social mores in order to find love and community.

The final major piece in my methodological framework is Linda Tuhiwai Smith's [41] *Decolonizing Methodologies*. Smith's detailing of how Indigenous knowledge has been suppressed, how the concept of research itself has been subverted and harnessed into mechanisms of colonialism, and what First Nations peoples have to offer in counter to this colonizing and colonized framework has been a crucial aspect of this project and others. Smith also draws on the way colonial methods of research have been used as a means of coercion and violence against other oppressed peoples, including Jews. Again and again, I have found comfort and solidarity in the writing of First Nations peoples, and wish to extend that solidarity back wherever possible. Smith also provides tools to challenge the supposed "objectivity" of (white) academia, to expose the ways so-called "truths" have been weaponized against people who exist in opposition and refusal to cisheteropatriarchal, white dominating, individualist, and classist modes of living. First Nations peoples, Jews, and queers have all existed, and continue to exist, in ways which undermine aristocracy and whiteness: living communally, sharing resources, focusing on community and environmental sustainability, challenging the notion of the nuclear family, and maintaining or building customs and spaces which are designed to question the status quo and reconnect with our bodies and those of others in a meaningful way, just to name a few.

The View from Inside-Outside

Before discussing recruitment, data collection, or any of the other practicalities of this study, it is crucial that I explicate the ways my methodological approach was affected by my own lived experience. The researcher is, after all, the acting force which puts all of these ideas into practice, and as such their positioning is arguably the most important material to draw into questioning. All the thinking explored in this chapter so far comes up distinctly against the position of the researcher as an objective observer of phenomenon; in other words, it is about questioning *the view from nowhere* [42], the notion that any one person (or even group of people) is able to accurately encompass and document some kind of "phenomenological truth" unburdened by localized or individual subjectivity [43]. This is not simply an intellectual shift but a targeted excavation of the embodied origin of thoughts and actions, an acknowledgement of the innate subjectivity of our lived existence [44].

Many of the counterpoints to the notion of objective observation lie in research on insider knowledge and insider-outsider research. As a queer butch Jew living in so-called Australia, I am placed squarely as what Hayfield and Huxley [45] define as "insider-outsider"; I am an insider by lived experience, but an outsider in the sense that each of us can never truly experience the inner world of another person or group. My presence as a researcher exploring, documenting, and analysing my own peoples is in itself a disruption to the classic "outsiders only" framework of settler-colonial academia [46]. This framework is constructed not only on the idea that "Others" in the settler-colonial academy do not have the capacity to conduct research appropriately but also that even those Others with access to these tools (e.g. academics with lived experience) cannot yield sufficiently "objective" and therefore rigorous research [47, 48].

Between the smart-but-untrustworthy or sometimes plainly evil stereotypes of Jewishness [49, 50], the so-called deviance and degeneracy often attributed to queerness [51, 52], and the abject monstrosity which transgender people have been tarred with for centuries [53]; it is easy to see how an uncritical observer who has swallowed these truths whole may object to my very presence in the academy. I have often been viewed and treated as "too inside" for much of my research. A great personal example of how all of these factors play out is in fact my very first research project, as part of my Psychological Science undergraduate degree, which one reviewer suggested to scrap entirely, as I was too close to my researched community (queer people). I later learned this reviewer's work was also largely based on old-school psychoanalysis, which in itself contains some unsavoury opinions of the supposed developmental stuckness of homosexuals [54, 55]. Somewhere between the Quest for Objectivity and some unresolved abjection of my personhood and that of my researched communities, my project was deemed too high risk. Needless to say, I persevered and succeeded in conducting my research. In some ways I am grateful for this early lesson in how the field of psychology and its home grounds of academia *et al.* view closeness and mutual identification. It allowed me to understand and question the displacement and rejection I felt, to shine a light on the biases of these supposedly objective, superior-in-hierarchy-only academics who do not see a benefit in considering the ways their lived experiences colour their work. It has allowed me to begin to unravel the ways in which we have all internalized these logics [56] and to view this process of internal decolonizing as a mitzvah [57], a part of my commitment to living Jewishly through self-betterment and the betterment of the world.

Critiques of insider-outsider research continue this line of thinking, by placing all issues associated with subjectivity squarely on people who belong to the communities they research. Some of these critiques include: the notion that shared community knowledge and assumptions around community customs and routines may prevent insiders-outsiders from delving in-depth into community narratives; the potential for "role confusion", wherein researchers may be seen as friends or even (heaven forbid) collaborators by their researched communities, thereby blurring the lines of professionalism which academia places as the gateway to objectivity; and the introduction of the supreme bugbear of empirical research, *bias* [48, 58–62]. The underlying assumption here is clear, being that distance and "professional" disengagement yield more accurate observations, and therefore a more "true" depiction of researched communities and their lived experience.

The actual truth, if I dare use that word, is much more complex for both supposed insiders and outsiders. While at a glance the description of the "risks" involved in insider research may seem like common sense, a second glance may reveal that each of these concerns is in fact a set of issues that are as likely to occur with outsiders as they do with insiders. No person, no matter their relationship to a person or community, is shielded from encountering these difficulties. The distinction between "insider issues" and "outsider issues" is largely dissolved when the discussion moves away from categorical belongingness and towards human connection and empathy. This is where I find myself today; while I am still engaged in research which looks into the specificities and deeper experiences of people with certain genders or sexualities, I am also working towards understanding the broader human experiences at play, and how our interconnectedness affects these more distinct experiences.

Each researcher exists at intersections of multiple axes of privilege, disadvantage, distance, and proximity, each of which is fluid and situational [63].

"Insideness", therefore, is not only a matter of category but a matter of connection. As Susan Gair [64] suggests, the core of good qualitative research (and arguably all research) is a sense of empathy, of building a project together from all the points of similarity and difference which exist between researchers and their researched communities. What may be positioned as objectivity, distance, or professionalism is in fact a denial of the significant rapport-building, community accountability, and development of insight and understanding of the researched communities which should underline all research which seeks to benefit that community [59, 64–66]. This is not to mention that for many people conducting insider research, the capacity to recruit from one's social circles is not only inevitable but also a crucial aspect of setting up a research relationship which can bring to fore deep, intimate, and often unspoken-of knowledge which a person or community may not trust a self-stated outsider to handle with the appropriate level of care [67–69]. This is part of what has driven me to move beyond the term "insider" or "insider-outsider"; instead, I view myself as what Megan Sharp [70] has termed *insighter*, someone who is both privy to community knowledge and who seeks to document, analyse, and ultimately bring greater visibility of my community's experiences through research.

Queer, Jewish, Decolonizing Methodologies in Practice

Having described the primary methodological underpinnings of my project, I will now turn to describing the ways these ideas have been applied throughout the project. Rather than listing the entire research protocol in the body of the paper, I have elected to provide it by request. Instead, I will discuss some of the important ways that my methodological frameworks have manifested in each of the study's method sections.

Recruitment and Interviewees

One of the first steps of any qualitative research projects is recruitment, and arguably even at this early point in the research process, there are already distinct opportunities to act radically. Rather than confining myself to any particular sampling approach, I decided to take full advantage of the benefits of insighter research by speaking to people whose relationship to me was at times significant and familiar [69], and at other times entirely new. The dynamics between my interviewees and myself ranged from people I had never met who responded to my online advertisement, through to friends of friends who were recommended to me, and all the way to people who had been my friends and colleagues, some for many years. This allowed for a fascinating oscillation between "the known and the nearly known" [71], between the depth facilitated by speaking with people in a way that did not require either party to "101 every term" [68] and the surprising or challenging perspectives which came up even in conversation with people who I was significantly familiar with.

While this sampling approach may seem ad-hoc, or even disorganized, it is in fact a distinct aspect of community research that deserves more recognition. Specifically, it is a negation of the notion of the visiting Researcher From Nowhere, a hazmat-suit-wearing scientist simply sent in to collect data at its purest most uninterrupted form and deliver it to the thesis, the journal article, or the policy report with as little contamination as possible. There is a real paranoia at hand here, a fear of "soiled" data or "unprofessional" relationships. Instead of succumbing to this paranoid approach, my recruitment methodology focused on reparative thinking [30], on opposing the abjection of subjectivity, and most importantly on the need for long-term investment in a community in order to truly represent its needs and utilize research for its benefit [72]. In that sense, it would be remiss of any researcher to disregard pre-existing long-term relationships simply because the academy exists under the long shadow of colonial "objectivity", an issue that has long been challenged by all three overarching methodological frameworks described above [73–75].

Data Collection

Interviews

Much of my methodological focus throughout the project has been on ensuring that interviews are conducted in a way that is not only safe(r) and comfortable for interviewees but is also oriented towards ensuring that my interviewees understood how their interviews contributed to my work more broadly. Firstly, interviewees nominated the time and place that was most convenient and comfortable for them to meet. Often this was in a café, or at the person's house, though for many interviewees the only communication options were phone or Skype, due to geographic distance or the interviewee's request. The interview process itself was kept intentionally semi-structured, in order for the conversation to be both flowing and not overly restricted in its focus. This meant that I was also allowing interviewees to discuss the areas which were important to them and to work with me on weaving some of those topics and experiences into a story [76], one which also contributed to the overarching narrative of the book. In many ways, this sense of collaborative inquiry was quite mutual [77]; at times I was surprised by a particular fact or perspective an interviewee brought up, and at other times interviewees commented that a particular question I had asked had never been brought to them before.

There was a genuine sense of a co-developed understanding throughout my interviews, an expansion of the notion of constructing knowledge hermeneutically "from within the language of one's own space" [78] which worked towards constructing a mutual lexicon. Several of my interviewees commented on the lack of need to code switch, or on how my understanding of a particular practice or set of Jewish and/or queer experiences smoothed out the interviewee's experience of expressing themself during our talk. Part of my process also involved ensuring that this sense of collaborative co-creating did not end when I switched off the recorder. I gave each interviewee the option to debrief, catch up again, and, perhaps most importantly, edit and approve the transcript, an action which is not always present in this style of research but which can significantly improve the quality of the data, as well as interviewees' sense of power and representation in the research process [68, 79, 80]. While this approach is less expedient[2], expediency as a goal of research could do with a re-evaluation; there are things that are lost when we rush and things which are gained when we slow down [81–83]. This is true both of interviews and analysis; there is a significant benefit to a "pedagogy of slowing down" [84], to treating the molasses of knowledge not as a non-Newtonian fluid to run across [85] but as a deep and sticky well to sink our hands into. In slowness we are better able to witness our surroundings, to understand the moment in all its complexities rather than sacrificing these details for the sake of pursuing the future or remaining mired in the past [86].

Other Data

A part of submerging myself into the aforementioned molasses has involved a bricolage of "official" and "informal" documentation and literature. The former was relatively straightforward: a Word document with dated journal entries and a set of iPhone notes where some inspirations were written down and used to guide the analysis process, as well as books and journal articles on my topics. The latter half, however, further plays with the boundaries of academia

---

2 Partly due to the nature of emails.

regarding what exactly "counts" as data. Throughout this process, some of the other points of data which I consider vital to the process included: casual unrecorded conversations regarding my developing analysis both with "insiders" and "outsiders"; zines; songs, albums, and my own musical outputs; and podcasts, just to name a few. This bricolage of methodologies and datapoints is partly intended to bring to the fore alternative and holistic ways of theorizing [87], ones which are personal, creative, embodied, and otherwise touching on expressions of knowledge which exist outside the written word [88].

Analysis

This methodological bricolage has also made its mark on the analysis process undertaken for this project. Partly, this was done as a refusal of the often restrictive nature of method [89], the bootstrapping of knowledge pursuit to static and pre-stated guidelines which form a rigid and unresponsive research structure, making "science subservient to method" as opposed to "liberating" the pursuit of knowledge and "let[ting] science be" [90]. In order to counteract this constraint, a significant factor in the project's analysis process was one of conversation, both about and with the data [91]. During this process, I also realized a significant flaw in how hermeneutics itself is often constructed. Namely, the notion of the hermeneutic cycle, the back-and-forth between reader and text, often fails to fully explain the transformative potential of hermeneutic reading. Within a cycle, the reader and the text remain separate entities, exchanging messages, often across time and space. Cycles are also steady, perfectly circular, and predictable.

Instead, I suggest that hermeneutic reading can lead to a kind of *swirling*; like stirring instant coffee into some water, or at times like being thrown into a rushing vortex with your choice of compatriot, bodies, and limbs becoming tough to distinguish in the gush. Things may start as a cycle, as a proverbial civil conversation between two separate parties (whether sentient or otherwise), but there is an inevitable enmeshment that takes place. As mentioned earlier in the paper, the hermeneutic cycle when used with the intention of developing deep understanding transforms both reader and text, but those transformations are not simply a development of new perspectives on a text or inner self-understanding but an internalizing experience of the cycle that is sticky and leaves traces of the material long after the "official" process of analysis is complete [92, 93]. Understanding oneself not simply as a *reader* contending with a *text* but, to paraphrase Kang (in Anderson 1996), as one of countless texts (in the broadest sense of the word) always swirling, swirling, swirling towards (methodological) freedom!

The analytical process in this project was therefore again a combination of "official" and "informal" analytical methods. The interview data was run through NVivo, where themes in interviews were clustered and labelled using Braun and Clarke's [95, 96] analysis guidelines. However, the "other" data was analysed in much more embodied and responsive ways; through conversations, opportunistic note-taking, immersion in creative outputs of Jews, queers, and queer Jews, and the "mulling over" of data in my mind and throughout my day. Although the analysis process is still ongoing at the time of writing this paper, NVivo-generated clusters will be supplemented by notes and experiences on all of the data involved. Not only have I *swirled* with a significant amount of other people's description of their lived experiences, as well as relevant (and sometimes irrelevant) literature, but also with my own lived experiences and history. This project sets objectivity aside in favour of producing a work that is analytically deep, personal, and taking on both the risks and benefits of "daring to be different" [97].

Dissemination

Dissemination strategies in most academic pursuits wind up in some predictable formats, namely peer-reviewed articles, books, and reports [98]. The academic system pushes for these types of publications, particularly the former, by incentivizing certain publication formats and perpetuating the "publish or perish" mentality so common within many academic disciplines [99, 100]. This is not to say that peer review is not crucial in many ways but rather that the focus on peer-reviewed publications detracts from what many researchers would classify as the actual goal of community research, being the community's benefit from any given study or project. Peer review right now, and for the last little while, is in many ways part of the "pen pal" approach discussed earlier: cumbersome and often lacking the immediacy and responsiveness which important data (and communities) deserve [101].

In order to circumvent some of these barriers to analysing and disseminating data, there was a need to consider more novel dissemination strategies [102]. I elected to give interviewees the option of having their interview published as part of a podcast series titled "Twice Blessed". Interviewees were provided with a separate podcast consent form and given the final say over the episode prior to its publication, including the opportunity to refuse publication. There was

a need to consider the audience and ensure that interviews were given suffi-
cient context so that a wide range of listeners could connect with the material.
I had reflected on what many of my interviewees had expressed to me, namely
the fact that most Australians, including many Jewish Australians, have little
to no understanding of the specifics of Judaism. This returns us to an earlier
point about the "risk" of assumed shared knowledge within insider/insighter
research. In order to counteract this gap, I spliced explanatory notes recorded
at the time of editing into each interview whenever a Jewish custom or term
was mentioned. This was kept as conversational and flowing to the rest of the
audio as possible while giving listeners (Jewish or gentile) the opportunity to
get a better understanding of our communities and language.

Podcasting is accessible to a much broader range of audiences than "traditional" academic methods by its very nature: most podcasts are mostly or
entirely free to listen to, downloadable, and pitched at a conversational level[3].
Meanwhile, most academic publications are stuck behind paywalls [103], contain opaque or inaccessible language [104], or are considered too intimidating
or prestigious to be engaged with for many people both outside and within
the academy [105]. However, my use of podcasting was not simply a matter
of releasing data early or quickly, or sidestepping the process of publication
entirely. Rather, it is in itself an extension of the methodologies described
throughout this book. Podcasting has the potential to fulfil a dual role, providing both a dissemination of pre-existing thoughts and analyses, as well as
a pedagogic methodology, which is intended to explore and highlight lived
experiences and marginalized perspectives which the general public may not
be exposed to [106].

Data in traditional publications is often dissected, "cleaned up", and presented as neat quotations for the reader. Wilson [40] suggests that this does a
disservice to both interviewee and researcher, and that interviews can only
be really delved into if the audience is provided with the whole conversation.
Researchers create data as much as their interviewees, and failing to include
this data leaves quotations and ideas lacking in context and depth. This is
not to say that podcasting exists *in opposition* to academic, text-based outputs,
but that it reiterates the notion of a researcher/writer/producer as a subjective
interpreter (and a subject of interpretation) rather than an objective scribe
[107]. There is also a vulnerability connected with podcasting, with hearing
audio voice recordings of people expressing their experiences, instead of the

---

3   This project also ensured the podcast was accessible to Deaf/Hard of Hearing people by
    providing a full transcript of each episode.

flattening effect of words on a page [108]. Timbre, pitch, accent, pacing, volume, and non-verbal sounds and silences all paint a picture which text alone can fall short of conveying [109]. Vulnerability on the part of podcast interviewees and/or hosts can also induce a sense of empathy in listeners, relying on the intimacy inherent in hearing a human voice and in the discussion of personal experiences, often within the context of broader themes [110].

Again, we see this sense of *swirling*, a messy and sticky oscillation between the experiences and contexts of the listener, the interviewee, and the researcher, whose roles cannot be fully disentangled from one another. This also means that even if only for a moment, the listener's sonic space is occupied by a voice that may have never entered their home otherwise [111]. That is radical in and of itself, this experience of a new voice in a person's domain, asking to be listened to. Podcasting as a publication strategy is therefore not only significant in terms of its availability but also in the way it ruptures the fourth wall, reminding listeners that they too are affected by the topics or experiences being discussed. And unlike manuscripts, listeners cannot help but have an embodied response, a sensory experience which continually reminds oneself that you are not dealing with words on a page but with a flesh and blood person and their perspectives [112].

This dissemination approach can also be understood as an extension of the ways that women and queer people challenge conservativism and religious fundamentalism within Jewishness through embodied practices [22, 113, 114]. We want our voices heard, and in order to do that we often have to forcibly occupy spaces which we have been prohibited from entering [115]. This includes occupying the position of cantor, Rabbi, or Talmud teacher, roles which rely primarily on not only using one's voice to convey one's perspectives and understandings but also ones which were entirely reserved for straight cisgender men until relatively recently [116]. The use of podcasting as a strategy is geared at queering the Eruv [117], the geographic private–public sacred space which practicing Jews remain within throughout Shabbat. It is positing that more voices are sacred and worthy of being heard than what old texts suggest and that more places deserve to have our experiences reverberate within than the inside of a Synagogue, if not the inside of a closet.

How to Read This Book

One notable point of difference in this book is my approach to presenting the interview data. Specifically, rather than writing up the usual call-and-response format utilized in much of qualitative research, I have decided to include interview tracts throughout this book as standalone pieces. The result of my analytical process is present through the writing which constitutes the main body of text, and I would like to provide readers with the opportunity to see how my interviewees' own words interact with my own personal analysis and consideration in a way that is more transparent. That is to say, rather than reducing the interviews to a singular, already-analysed, and pre-digested form, I am taking the approach favoured by many Talmudic texts.

Texts overlap, come apart, and are presented as separate but interacting voices which touch, however, never congeal into each other. Rather, like commentary on religious texts, the reader is provided with all points of view. You may find the point of discussion where a particular quote is placed to be poignant and apt – you may also find it jarring or confusing. This is the by-product of the self-determination and autonomy I am trying to provide to both myself and my interviewees; by leaving certain connections unspoken, hinted-towards, or otherwise open to interpretation, my intention is to not have my words in this book be cast as the final say on whichever topic is being discussed. Rather, as with Talmud or any other interpretative text, I am aware that other people (including those who I interviewed for this project) may have different points of view or opinions from me on any given subject. Disagreement has always been an aspect of Jewish textual interpretation and understanding, in particular [118], and I intend to honour this tradition through this book's presentation of different voices. By adding interview tracts as commentary boxes (and podcast interviews, as discussed above), I am attempting to give all participating parties (myself, the interviewees, and the reader) the freedom of having their own position stated – even if freedom is at times more costly than we would like it to be [119].

And so, dear reader, consider the proceeding chapters to be the voices of many, not just a singular interpretation by one. I have done my best to honour my interviewees and to allow their perspectives and experiences to affect how I witness the emerging themes and concepts that I detail in this book. However, it is also up to you to consider where there are points of convergence or ambiguity, and to immerse in those potentially complicated emotions just as I did when writing this text. Maybe you won't agree with a single word I have written – maybe it will all read like an illuminated book. I expect neither outcome but welcome both, in humility and openness.

Conclusion

Queer, Jewish, and decolonizing methodologies all have significant potential to inspire radical and non-traditional approaches to research with marginalized peoples. The application of these methodologies throughout this project is just one way to deploy these methodologizations of lived experiences and intergenerational knowledge. While there are many "risks" associated with utilizing more intimate, subjective, and bricolage tools when collecting data, there are also significant benefits. This is particularly true of utilizing alternative routes to knowledge dissemination which question the role and usefulness of academic publication traditions. These methodologies are also effective in facilitating an embodied understanding of knowledge, one that can be internally, relationally, and possibly structurally transformative for anyone who is willing to listen.

References

[1] Rojtman B. *Black Fire on White Fire: An Essay on Jewish Hermeneutics, from Midrash to Kabbalah*. University of California Press, 1998.

[2] Diamond JA. The questioning Jew and the Jewish question. *CrossCurrents* 2014; 64: 123–130.

[3] Karo RY. Halakhah, Shulchan Arukh | Sefaria, <https://www.sefa ria.org/texts/Halak hah/Shulchan> Arukh (1565, accessed 21 July 2020).

[4] Sigel IE, Kress JS, Elias MJ. Beyond questioning: Inquiry strategies and cognitive and affective elements of Jewish education. *J Jew Educ* 2007; 73: 51–66.

[5] Veltri G. *Alienated Wisdom: Enquiry into Jewish Philosophy and Scepticism*. Walter de Gruyter GmbH & Co KG, 2018.

[6] Drinkwater G, Lesser J, Shneer D. *Torah Queeries: Weekly Commentaries on the Hebrew Bible*. NYU Press, 2012.

[7] Sienna N. *A Rainbow Thread: An Anthology of Queer Jewish Texts from the First Century To 1969*. Print-O-Craft LLC, 2019.

[8] Rosenthal RS. Of pearls and fish: An analysis of Jewish legal texts on sexuality and their significance for contemporary American Jewish movements. *Columbia J Gend Law* 2006; 15: 485–541.

[9] Shahak I. *Jewish Fundamentalism in Israel*. London, UK: Pluto Press, 2004.

[10] Lazar A, Hammer JH. Religiousness and anti-gay/lesbian attitudes: The mediating function of intratextual religious fundamentalism. *Psychol Violence* 2018; 8: 763–771.

[11] Ansara YG. Beyond cisgenderism: Counselling people with non-assigned gender identities. In: *Counselling Ideologies: Queer Challenges to Heteronormativity*. 2010, pp. 167–200.

[12] Hartal G, Sasson-Levy O. ReReading Homonationalism: An Israeli Spatial Perspective. *J Homosex* 2017; 65(10): 1–24.

[13] Levon E. The voice of others: Identity, alterity and gender normativity among gay men in Israel. *Lang Soc* 2012; 41: 187–211.

[14] Shilo G, Antebi N, Mor Z. Individual and community resilience factors among lesbian, gay, bisexual, queer and questioning youth and adults in Israel. *Am J Community Psychol* 2015; 55: 215–227.

[15] Shlomo G. The Jewish Queer Continuum in Yeshiva Narratives. *Shofar* 2017; 35: 1–31.

[16] Torah T. Who We Are, <http://transtorah.org/> (2018).

[17] Graham D, Markus A. *Gen17 Australian Jewish Community Survey: Preliminary Findings.* Monash University: Australian Centre for Jewish Civilisation, 2017.

[18] Ruttenberg D. *The Passionate Torah: Sex and Judaism.* NYU Press, 2009.

[19] Diamond JA. *Converts, Heretics, and Lepers: Maimonides and the Outsider.* University of Notre Dame Press, 2007.

[20] Held BS. Epistemic violence in psychological science: Can knowledge of, from, and for the (othered) people solve the problem? *Theory Psychol* 2020; 30: 349–370.

[21] Teo T. What is epistemological violence in the empirical social sciences? *Soc Personal Psychol Compass* 2010; 4: 295–303.

[22] Rosenberg S. "Lehadlik": Radical Jewish music, gender and disidentification in Aviva Endean's work. *Dir New Music* 2018; 2: 1–12.

[23] Boyarin D. *Sparks of the Logos: Essays in Rabbinic Hermeneutics.* Brill, <https://books.goo gle.com.au/books?id=i8IzSyQZTW0C> (2003).

[24] Crome A. Hermeneutics and the Jews in Protestant thought. In: Crome A (ed). *The Restoration of the Jews: Early Modern Hermeneutics, Eschatology, and National Identity in the Works of Thomas Brightman.* Cham: Springer International Publishing, pp. 29–58.

[25] Wolfson ER. *Along the Path: Studies in Kabbalistic Myth, Symbolism, and Hermeneutics.* SUNY Press, 2012.

[26] Wolfson ER. *Language, Eros, Being: Kabbalistic Hermeneutics and Poetic Imagination.* Fordham Univ Press, 2009.

[27] Gadamer HG. *Truth and Method.* USA: Seabury Press, 1975.

[28] Hall DE. *Reading Sexualities: Hermeneutic Theory and the Future of Queer Studies.* Routledge, 2009.

[29] Anderson D. *Text & Sex.* NSW: Random House Australia, 1995.

[30] Sedgwick EK. *Touching Feeling: Affect, Pedagogy, Performativity.* Duke University Press, 2003.

[31] Haeberle EJ. The Jewish contribution to the development of sexology. *J Sex Res* 1982; 18: 305–323.

[32] Plant R. *The Pink Triangle: The Nazi War Against Homosexuals.* New York: Henry Holt and Company, 2011.

[33] Setterington K. *Branded by the Pink Triangle.* Toronto, Ontario: Second Story Press, 2013.

[34] Whisnant C. *Queer Identities and Politics in Germany: A History, 1880–1945.* New York: Harrington Park Press, 2016.

[35] Jakobsen JR. Queers are like Jews, aren't they? Analogy and alliance politics. *Queer Theory and the Jewish Question* 2003; 64–89.

[36] Noyman B. מרחב גוף שפה / ראיית העולם הנאצית (*The Nazi Worldview / Space Body Language*). University of Haifa, /products/book-14821 (2002, accessed 27 July 2020).

[37] Tatz C. An essay in disappointment: the Aboriginal–Jewish relationship. *Aborig Hist* 2004; 28: 100–121.

[38] Abdo N, Yuval-Davis N. Palestine, Israel and the Zionist settler project. *Unsettling Settl Soc Articul Gend Race Ethn Cl* 1995; 11: 291–322.

[39] Ghanem A, Mustafa M. The Palestinians in Israel: The Challenge of the Indigenous Group Politics in the "Jewish State". *J Muslim Minor Aff* 2011; 31: 177–196.

[40] Wilson S. *Research Is Ceremony: Indigenous Research Methods*. Canada: Fernwood Publishing, 2008.

[41] Smith LT. *Decolonizing Methodologies: Research and Indigenous Peoples*. 2nd ed. London, United Kingdom: Zed Books, 2012.

[42] Nagel T. *The View from Nowhere*. Oxford University Press, USA, 1989.

[43] Shapin S. Placing the view from nowhere: Historical and sociological problems in the location of science. *Trans Inst Br Geogr* 1998; 23: 5–12.

[44] Orbán K. A view from nowhere: The zero perspective view of bodily awareness. *Teorema Rev Int Filos* 2018; 37: 39–64.

[45] Hayfield N, Huxley C. Insider and outsider perspectives: Reflections on researcher identities in research with lesbian and bisexual women. *Qual Res Psychol* 2015; 12: 91–106.

[46] Beals F, Kidman J, Funaki H. Insider and outsider research: Negotiating self at the edge of the Emic/Etic divide. *Qual Inq* 2020; 26: 593–601.

[47] Doulatram DN. Indigenous decolonization of academia: Using the Marshall Islands as precedent for social injustice. *J Humanit Cult Stud RD* 2016; 3: 1–48.

[48] Toy-Cronin B. Ethical issues in insider-outsider research. *SAGE Handb Qual Res Ethics* 2018; 1: 455–468.

[49] Biberman M. *Masculinity, Anti-Semitism and Early Modern English Literature: From the Satanic to the Effeminate Jew*. Routledge, 2017.

[50] Helmreich W. *The Things They Say behind Your Back: Stereotypes and the Myths Behind Them*. Routledge, 2017.

[51] Bullough VL. *Homosexuality: A History (from Ancient Greece to Gay Liberation)*. Routledge, 2019.

[52] Warner M. *The Trouble with Normal: Sex, Politics, and the Ethics of Queer Life*. Harvard University Press, 2000.

[53] Stryker S. *Transgender History*. Seal Press, 2008.

[54] Kunzel R. The "durable homophobia" of psychoanalysis. *Mod Intellect Hist* 2020; 17: 215–219.

[55] Shapira M. The new history of psychoanalysis: Towards a richer and more nuanced narrative. *Mod Intellect Hist* 2020; 17: 227–231.

[56] Tuitt F. Disrupting the Colonial Gaze. *Decolonizing Qual Approaches Caribb* 2019; 205.

[57] Satlow ML. *Creating Judaism: History, Tradition, Practice*. Columbia University Press, 2006.

[58] Asselin EM. Insider research: Issues to consider when doing qualitative research in your own setting. *J Nurses Staff Dev JNSD* 2003; 19: 99–103.

[59] Breen LJ. The researcher "in the middle": Negotiating the insider/outsider dichotomy. *Aust Community Psychol* 2007; 19: 163–174.

[60] Brewis J. The Ethics of Researching Friends: On Convenience Sampling in Qualitative Management and Organization Studies. *Br J Manag* 2014; 25: 849–862.

[61] Kanuha V. "Being" native versus "going native": Conducting social work research as an insider. *Soc Work* 2000; 45: 439–447.

[62] Unluer S. Being an insider researcher while conducting case study research. *Qual Rep*; 17, <https://eric.ed.gov/?id=EJ981455> (2012, accessed 3 August 2020).

[63] Dhillon JK, Thomas N. Ethics of engagement and insider-outsider perspectives: issues and dilemmas in cross-cultural interpretation. *Int J Res Method Educ* 2019; 42: 442–453.

[64] Gair S. Feeling their stories: Contemplating empathy, insider/outsider positionings, and enriching qualitative research. *Qual Health Res* 2012; 22: 134–143.

[65] Humphrey C. Insider-outsider: Activating the hyphen. *Action Res* 2007; 5: 11–26.

[66] Mayrl D, Westbrook L. On writing public sociology: Accountability through accessibility, dialogue, and relevance. In: Jeffries V (ed). *Handbook of Public Sociology*. Washington, DC: Rowman & Littlefield Publishers, 2009.

[67] Kerstetter K. Insider, outsider, or somewhere between: The impact of researchers' identities on the community-based research process. *J Rural Soc Sci*; 27, <https://egrove.olemiss.edu/jrss/vol27/iss2/7> (2012).

[68] Rosenberg S, Tilley PJM. "A Point of Reference": The insider-outsider research staircase and transgender people's experiences of participating in trans-led research. *Qual Res* 2020; 21(6), 923–938.

[69] Taylor J. The intimate insider: Negotiating the ethics of friendship when doing insider research. *Qual Res* 2011; 11: 3–22.

[70] Sharp M. "Insighters": The complexity of qualitative methods in youth music research. *J Youth Stud* 2020; 0: 1–16.

[71] Cook T. The purpose of mess in action research: Building rigour though a messy turn. *Educ Action Res* 2009; 17: 277–291.

[72] Wallerstein N, Duran B. Community-based participatory research contributions to intervention research: The intersection of science and practice to improve health equity. *Am J Public Health* 2010; 100: S40–S46.

[73] Allen A. *The End of Progress: Decolonizing the Normative Foundations of Critical Theory*. Columbia University Press, 2016.

[74] Dilley P. Queer theory: Under construction. *Int J Qual Stud Educ* 1999; 12: 457–472.

[75] Morgan ML. *Interim Judaism: Jewish thought in a century of crisis*. Indiana University Press, 2001.

[76] Kovach M. Conversational method in Indigenous research. *First Peoples Child Fam Rev* 2010; 5 (1): 40–48.

[77] Caraballo L, Lyiscott J. Collaborative inquiry: Youth, social action, and critical qualitative research. *Action Res* 2020; 18: 194–211.

[78] Smith DG. Hermeneutic inquiry: The hermeneutic imagination and the pedagogic text. *Forms Curric Inq* 1991; 3: 187–210.

[79] Mero-Jaffe I. "Is that what I Said?" Interview transcript approval by participants: An aspect of ethics in qualitative research. *Int J Qual Methods* 2011; 10: 231–247.

[80] Thomas DR. Feedback from research participants: Are member checks useful in qualitative research? *Qual Res Psychol* 2017; 14: 23–41.

[81] Bressers G, Brydges M, Paradis E. Ethnography in health professions education: Slowing down and thinking deeply. *Med Educ* 2020; 54: 225–233.

[82] Clandinin DJ, Caine V, Lessard S. *The Relational Ethics of Narrative Inquiry*. Routledge, 2018.

[83] Lessard S, Kootenay I, Whiskeyjack F, et al. Working with indigenous elders in narrative inquiry: Reflections and key considerations. *Qual Inq* 2020; 27(1), 28–36. 1077800419898498.

[84] Kanarek J. The pedagogy of slowing down: Teaching Talmud in a Summer Kollel. *Teach Theol Relig* 2010; 13: 15–34.

[85] Choudhary Vivek. Fun with Non-Newtonian Fluid – Lamar University, <https://www.youtube.com/watch?v=RIUEZ3AhrVE> (2014, accessed 17 August 2020).

[86] Rose DB. Slowly~writing into the Anthropocene. *TEXT* 2013; 17: 1–14.

[87] Tobin K. Methodological bricolage. *Eventful Learn* 2018; 31–55.

[88] O'Brien S. Thinking through moving image and performance. In: Engels-Schwarzpaul AChr, Peters MA (eds). *Of Other Thoughts: Non-Traditional Ways to the Doctorate: A Guidebook for Candidates and Supervisors*. UK: Springer Science & Business Media, 2013, 1, pp. 221–238.

[89] Feyerabend P. *Against Method*. Verso, 2010.

[90] Caputo JD. *Radical Hermeneutics: Repetition, Deconstruction, and the Hermeneutic Project*. Indiana University Press, 1988.

[91] Rapley T. *Doing Conversation, Discourse and Document Analysis*. SAGE, 2018.

[92] Ahmed S. *Cultural Politics of Emotion*. Edinburgh University Press, 2014.

[93] Ardoin P, McWilliam F. Introduction: On the stickiness of the short story and the cycle. *J Short Story Engl Cah Nouv* 2016; 21–29.

[94] Anderson MB. Treehouse of Horror VII. *The Simpsons*.

[95] Braun V, Clarke V. Using thematic analysis in psychology. *Qual Res Psychol* 2006; 3: 77–101.

[96] Braun V, Clarke V. *Successful Qualitative Research: A Practical Guide for Beginners*. Newbury Park, California: SAGE Publishing, 2013.

[97] Cardno C, Rosales-Anderson N, McDonald M. Documentary analysis hui: An emergent bricolage method for culturally responsive qualitative research. Epub ahead of print 2017. DOI: 10.20507/MAIJournal.2017.6.2.4.

[98] Bluemke DA, Sosna J. Peer-reviewed publications in 2020: Still needed? *Radiology* 2020; 295: 495–495.

[99] Moosa IA. *Publish or Perish: Perceived Benefits versus Unintended Consequences*. Edward Elgar Publishing, 2018.

[100] Neff MW. Publication incentives undermine the utility of science: Ecological research in Mexico. *Sci Public Policy* 2018; 45: 191–201.

[101] Huisman J, Smits J. Duration and quality of the peer review process: The author's perspective. *Scientometrics* 2017; 113: 633–650.

[102] Bullock R, Gooch D, Little M, et al. *Research in Practice: Experiments in Development and Information Design*. Routledge, 2018.

[103] James JE. Pirate open access as electronic civil disobedience: Is it ethical to breach the paywalls of monetized academic publishing? *J Assoc Inf Sci Technol*; n/a. Epub ahead of print 2020. DOI: 10.1002/asi.24351.

[104] Thursby M, Kimberley E. Framing the text: Understanding emotional barriers to academic reading. *J Univ Teach Learn Pract* 2020; 17: 1–12.

[105] Carter S. Academia as unhomely habitus? In: Carter S (ed). *Academic Identity and the Place of Stories: The Personal in the Professional*. Cham: Springer International Publishing, pp. 35–54.

[106] Richardson S, Green H. Talking women/women talking: The feminist potential of podcasting for modernist studies. *Fem Mod Stud* 2018; 1: 282–293.

[107] Llinares D. Podcasting as liminal praxis: Aural mediation, sound writing and identity. In: Llinares D, Fox N, Berry R (eds). *Podcasting: New Aural Cultures and Digital Media*. Cham: Springer International Publishing, pp. 123–145.

[108] Lindgren M. Personal narrative journalism and podcasting. *Radio JournalInternational Stud Broadcast Audio Media* 2016; 14: 23–41.

[109] Harter LM. Storytelling in acoustic spaces: Podcasting as embodied and engaged scholarship. *Health Commun* 2019; 34: 125–129.

[110] Spinelli M, Dann L. *Podcasting: The Audio Media Revolution*. Bloomsbury Publishing USA, 2019.

[111] Tiffe R, Hoffmann M. Taking up sonic space: Feminized vocality and podcasting as resistance. *Fem Media Stud* 2017; 17: 115–118.

[112] Copeland S. A feminist materialisation of amplified voice: Queering identity and affect in the heart. In: Llinares D, Fox N, Berry R (eds). *Podcasting: New Aural Cultures and Digital Media*. UK: Springer, 2018, pp. 209–226.

[113] Benjamin MH. Tracing the contours of a half century of Jewish feminist theology. *J Fem Stud Relig* 2020; 36: 11–31.

[114] Milligan AK. *Jewish Bodylore: Feminist and Queer Ethnographies of Folk Practices*. Rowman & Littlefield, 2018.

[115] Milligan A. Chapter twelve: The subversive Jewish feminist body: Creating spaces of protest through embodiment insynagogue life. *Mak Gend Intersect Hum Divine* 2019; 219.

[116] Hauptman J. *Rereading the Rabbis: A Woman's Voice*. Routledge, 2019.

[117] Kahn JM. Queer Eruv. *IMAGES* 2011; 5: 61–65.

[118] Dolgopolski S. *What Is Talmud?: The Art of Disagreement*. Fordham University Press. Epub ahead of print 25 August 2009. DOI: 10.1515/9780823238767.

[119] MacCallum GC. Negative and positive freedom. In: *The Liberty Reader*. Routledge, 2017, pp. 100–122.

· 2 ·

HERENESS AND COMMUNITY

In order to understand queer Jewish experiences, the most central starting point is often that of community. There are myriad 'here's that are worthy of exploring, each providing different perspectives on the kind of community experiences one might encounter as a queer Jew in Australia. The majority of (certainly mainstream) writing on both Jews and queers takes a monolithic approach to the notion of "community", often ignoring the ways specific geographies, relationships, and political histories form unique communities and sub-communities. Delving into the inherent fragmentation and natural diversity within each of these communities tells much more complex and fascinating stories than any singular story of a Jewish Community™ or LGBTQIA+ Community™ ever could. This chapter explores how different 'here's interplay with the lived experiences of queer Jewish people living in so-called Australia.

Land and Country

"I've never really felt as though I should be here in Australia. I think what happened here was really disgusting. And I still occupy this land with my body, as do my family."
– Ariel

It is impossible (or perhaps irresponsible, more accurately) to delve into human experiences without first considering the lands we live on. This is particularly true with the topic of this book; the relationship between Jews and land is one of flux, of oscillation between digging our heels in and fleeing elsewhere to (supposed) safety. The violent spectre of the state of Israel[1] haunts and distorts one of the core tenets of Jewish life, that of remaining responsive to the land and others living on it. We are often compelled by our traditions and ethics to respond to the needs of the land and its inhabitants, whether through direct action or ritual; to celebrate what is plentiful and revive what is wilting; to honour the sustenance which the earth gives us; and to feel changes in the air and respond in turn. This is more complex for Jews living in the Southern hemisphere, where summer Holy Days are celebrated in the dead of winter and seasonal shifts are often misaligned with the Jewish calendar. Nonetheless, we are encouraged to immerse in the movement of seasons, in the cycles of the moon and of the vegetation and of each passing day.

However, this notion of responsivity to land is transformed significantly within the context of contemporary so-called Australia[2]. Here, the land is not politically neutral[3]; it is land that has been violently[4] taken away from Traditional Owners and First Nations communities, catalysing significant intergenerational trauma and disrupting connections to Country which form a vital aspect of Aboriginal life and wellbeing [1]. If I am to write about my communities, and the lands they are situated on, it is imperative that I name Aboriginal genocide and its lingering impacts on First Nations peoples. This is not a matter of acknowledgement, however; this is a matter of fact – a fact of great importance which affects all Jews living on these stolen lands, whether or not they choose to acknowledge it as such. The history of Jewish people is one so heavily narrativized around nomadism, diaspora, and movement, and rarely taking roots in one place, to such an extent that we as Jews do not have the vocabulary to comprehend such a deep uninterrupted connection to land.

There is an urge to draw comparisons here, namely between Jews' supposed "return" to their ancestral Levant after centuries of exile and Aboriginals'

---

1 And the significant internalization of that regime's propaganda by Jews in Israel and globally.

2 The term "so-called" is used here to denote that Australia is *not* a singular white Christian colony but rather a continent housing hundreds of tribes, clans, and their distinct territories which cannot be neatly summarized under a singular national identity or title.

3 It rarely is.

4 Or more accurately, genocidally.

claims to Native Title [2]. But we must resist that urge. At their core, Jew-ish thought, culture, and traditions do not have direct equivalences with the depth and continuity of relationship to Country that First Nations cultures and peoples in so-called Australia and elsewhere[5] have. The overwhelming majority of Jews are exiled peoples, often unable to stay in one place for more than a handful of generations; how could we possibly comprehend the unin-terrupted intergenerational knowledge of a land that spans hundreds of genera-tions? If climate change (and the Indigenous-led movements formed to counter it) has taught us anything, it's that a deep understanding of Country cannot be achieved through colonialist and Anglicized means of knowledge production, such as institutionalized research, no matter how many years or decades any particular project spans[3, 4]. Country is understood through stories, through immersion, through a sense of not only responsivity but *responsibility* to land, environment, and the life existing within them; these perspectives form an integral part of Aboriginal connection to land and are often suppressed in favour of more "western" approaches to environment [5, 6].

In order to move forward with this book, it is imperative that we address our conception of Jewish exile head-on. Specifically, it is vital to enquire into this obsession with *landedness*, with a kind of *return to ancestral soil* that is seen as wholly positive to such an extent that we seem to have no choice but to demonize its counterpart in the diaspora. Land ownership, or lack thereof, is hard-wired into the Jewish narrative – from Pogroms and ostracization to the rubberband effects in the early twentieth century which led to an ever-hardening stance of the need for a Jewish state, by any means necessary. There is a trickle-down of binaries at play here: *Zion/Diaspora*, which carries the implication of *landedness/landlessness*, which in turn activates perhaps one of the most visceral binaries which every human being wrangles with across their lifetime, that of *togetherness/aloneness* [7]. The narrative of Jews and land is one of dispersal, of splintering away from a singular centre, and of a forced forfei-ture which repeats with alarming regularity. This narrative is inherently trau-matic, with heavy themes of separation, rejection, struggle, and often death. It seems only fair for a traumatized peoples to buck against that pressure, resist those personal or collective psychic events, and return to an earlier (read: bet-ter) time [8]. This is most obviously reflected in the logics around the state of Israel's positioning as a reclamation of the land of Canaan, where Jews existed prior to our most primordial exile [9]. Israel is a comfort blanket, a kind of

5 Including Palestine.

collective salve against generational trauma which spans centuries, a *return* to a time before that most fundamental and traumatic psychic event of diaspora.

However, as Catherine Malabou [10] suggests, significant trauma often causes irrevocable disruption to identity, in a kind of violent *flash* which permanently alters a person to such an extent that they may not even recognize themselves. We can extend this logic onwards from individuals to groups, particularly groups who have been subjected to such cumulative trauma. Specifically, it would be impossible for Jewish Personhood to remain psychologically intact through such persistent persecution, violence, and genocide. You don't need to look any further than the diaspora narrative to understand the ways in which we keep our most violent collective experiences alive, mulling them over at every Holy Day, joking that "they tried to kill us, they failed, let's eat". "They" may have failed to kill us all, but they certainly killed plenty, and the rest of us live to tell ourselves the tales every single year. Unfortunately, we have been led to believe that the tale ends in safety, specifically through the Israeli nation-state: there, Jewish people will no longer face persecution, and can return to our ancestral lands. But if the persistent and arguably increasing rates of (particularly anti-Black) racism [11], pro-Ashkenazi colourism [12], queerphobia [13], and division between the poor and the rich [14] in Israel are anything to go by, this nation's capacity to protect against further Jewish trauma is closer to a blankie than a fortress in its efficacy.

Dahni: I find ideas of belonging around being Australian really interesting, particularly in some of the conversations and the dynamics that are going on in this country at the moment.
I do [belong] because it's where I live and it's my citizenship. But I don't necessarily know what that means

Settler-colonial nation-states rely on self-cannibalism, on a shadow group which bolsters the superiority of those groups allowed into sunlight, a process which relies on those "superior" groups ignoring if not bulldozing any trace of their broader shared humanity and equal right to live. After all, colonization by its very nature relies on an uninterrupted and unchallenged hegemony, which is directly contradicted by cultural and societal pluralism [15]. This shadow group will suffer violence and oppression until it no longer serves a purpose; as Veracini [16] highlights, the ultimate aim of a settler-colonial project such as Israel is to "indigenize" its colonizing people to the land, meaning that the land's legitimate indigenous inhabitants must be either assimilated or completely wiped out. There can be no voice of dissent, or pockets of resistance, for the settler-colonial project to be complete because the narrative of indigeneity does not accommodate any stories other than ones of uninterrupted and unmitigated belonging to a land. But the history of Jews is undeniably one of interruption, of dispossession. It is not "whole" in its connection to any land, though our peoples have in fact deeply connected to many lands at one point or another. But this matter of repeated trauma and our collective processing of that trauma must be tackled head-on in order to move forward.

If we were to understand communities as bodies, then we can see how severely scarred the Collective Jewish Body is. Whether by the lashes of the world or our own drive to gnaw our legs out of a proverbial steel trap, the Collective Jewish Body carries keloids and cicatrices, not to mention those open wounds which operate more like ports, permanently exposed, embodying the volatile balance between curative exchanges and increased risk of infection. This Body has been consumed, violated, and most horrifically, turned against itself. This latter violence is perpetuated by many means, such as internalized antisemitism, other markers of division such as class or gender, or the twisting and dazzling outcomes of divisive, cynical, and often banal political propaganda. But perhaps most harmful of all is the overarching narrative told by this Body to itself: that there is a way back, that a person[6] can undo significant harm and revert to a healthier, safer, or otherwise less destabilized version of themself. But unfortunately for those who feel emboldened by (and compelled to perpetuate) this narrative, nothing could be further from the truth.

Malabou and Miller's conception of an *identity without precedent* [8] illuminates the paradox inherent in attempting to understand personhood following significant trauma. There is no full recovery here, nor any kind of collective time travel that undoes anti-Jewish atrocities and their impact on us as a whole. The Collective Jewish Body has been afflicted, creating a new Body, and an Identity within it, who may have similarities to their past iterations but are ultimately *without precedent* in terms of how this Body/Person navigates the world and understands itself. Those outside the trauma may try to make sense of this new person by forming mental links between the pre- and post-incident person, attempting to eke out connective tissue, no matter how thin. This act is bound to produce tension and frustration, particularly if the person's personality or way of living in the world has changed in ways which cannot be ignored day to day. Those inside the trauma are navigating a double burden: being forced to articulate their lived experiences and the effects of those experiences on their personhood, all while having undergone such a radical transformation

---

6 Here used to mean either individual or the Collective Jewish Body.

that any chance of self-recognition may have been entirely ameliorated. We want to quell confusion, to ensure that there is some cohesive narrative tying one day to the next, connecting each person to themselves, an uncut thread. But it is a Sisyphean task to attempt to glue a fine day to a horrible day, an unaffected person to an affected person, to thumb the seam formed by an *event* in an attempt to squish two halves of clay into a singular piece. The clay now has stains, trace elements, hard rocks, and sometimes even clumps of new matter so large they entirely usurp the original material. Reversal is impossible, and we must contend with what is materially in our hands; something less "pure", but still malleable, and arguably even more fascinating than before.

It is exactly this fascination which brings the discussion back to Jews and land. Even within relatively recent history, there is evidence that many Jewish communities were proponents of non-territorial autonomy, favouring community survival and thriving over notions of safety and culture growth through nationhood and land-based wealth generation [17, 18]. Modern writers such as JB Brager [19] and Kamil Kijek [20] explore how this perspective extends to modern-day politics about land in occupied Palestine and elsewhere, particularly using the lens of *doykeit (hereness)*. Thinking of one's *hereness* opens up alternative narrative pathways to the narrative of *awayness* that is commonly associated with diaspora living. This is where Zionism shows itself for the atrophying force that it is, in foisting a sense of *awayness*, of isolation, of incompleteness, upon all those Jews who either do not live in, or outright reject the legitimacy of, the state of Israel. Even the most fervent Zionist, unless living in the so-called Holy Land, is bound for a life of lack and longing by the very nature of their belief: that we all belong in a singular place, and that this place is our only guaranteed bastion of safety, deep connection, and religious wholeness. But how can we be away from a place that does not exist?

There is a sense of manufactured desperation underlying these square-peg-round-hole attempts at selling Jews on this notion of Zion/Israel as our sole *homeland*. It's a kind of *magical nationalism*, an understanding of land

Madelaine: I try to explain to non Jews that Israel is a place but it's also a place that's in every part of the Talmud and every part that you read you are a child of Israel. It's not just a place. And [...] that's woven into your identity. I didn't go there and feel like I'd come home but I did feel very comfortable. Having my aunt meet me there with falafel at the airport definitely helped that. But also the Israeli government is horrendous, and they're committing crimes and they're acting in ways that Jews have been treated and they're acting that upon Palestinians. and it's like, how do I feel connected to a place that's even more abhorrent and right wing than the politics that I live in now?

ownership and ethno-religious cohesion that is rooted in myths, historical tracts of varying levels of authenticity and relevance, and human interpretations of "divine" texts [21]. Conversely, this *magical nationalism* is, by intention, divorced from the facts of the land; it turns genocide into self-protection, annexation into a legitimate means of survival and cruelty, and violence into archetypal stories of bravery and struggle. It is a promise that is perpetually resting gently on the horizon, urging us to fruitlessly make our way towards it while threatening to vanish over the edge of the world. It is asking us to *look away* from something while moving towards it, transmogrifying blood and tears into milk and honey, an oasis that turns into a mirage again and again and again [22, 23].

We can only resist these illusions by grounding ourselves, by looking around us and seeing what is already *here*. We are not only being asked to look away from the horrors of the Israeli apartheid state, or the exclusionary and prejudiced mechanics buried deep within our culture but we are also being asked to look away from the lived reality of Jewish peoples across the world. We can look at the Jewish story as one of escape and forced removal and mass violence and death, but we are missing those radical aspects which underline each of these experiences: our ability to adapt, to withstand, to maintain our knowledge and traditions and ways of being through even the most horrific of events. We take forces exerted upon us and karate them back onto our oppressors. We survive and thrive almost as a revenge, existing in spite of attempts to either banish us from a land or assimilate us so fully into it that we forget who we are. We move like seeds in the wind, growing where we can, regardless of whether we ourselves or our progeny are then uprooted or forced away by strong gales.

Margie: I was quite political [in my opinion] that Israel probably shouldn't exist even though Jews had been exterminated. And on the one hand, I really believed in a safe place. Remember this [. . .] was around the seven day war. I believe that it should be a safe place, but also [that] it actually was going to be a great big disaster. And what about Palestinians? And how could you put Israel in amongst a whole lot of anti-Semitic people and think it was going to be all right?

Jewish tactics of survival are not exemplified by Wall and Tower [24], by land grab or other offensive manoeuvres which displace others. We survive the way we always have: by keeping the people and their cultures alive and well, wherever they may be [25]. Our power does not emanate from a piece of land or the ligatures of religious fundamentalism but rather the very fact of our dispersal. It would be difficult to engage with *doykeit* and its sociopolitical implications without considering the through-lines between Jewish life and anarchism. Jews are decentralized in our geographic locations, compelled towards mutual aid and community support by the tenets of our beliefs and culture, and nearly always at odds with broader oppressive authoritarian powers which enact violence against us and other persecuted peoples [26]. *This* is the legacy that is being denied to us over this obsession with *landedness*, with possessiveness and the story of instability and fear as its explanatory framework. Land and possessions have never given us safety. We have only ever been (as) safe (as possible) when we have remained invested firmly in the needs of our communities, and when we've refused to supplant the strength each Jewish person yields from within themselves and their community in favour of a single power source (e.g. Israel or any other nation-state or regime). When we stop dreaming of a perfect land for the Jewish people, we can wake up to the capacities and responsibilities we already have, and the complexity and necessity of actions to make *here*, wherever that may be, a better place for all.

Here: Australia

Dahni: I have this thing, I don't really identify as white even though I kind of am, but I'm kind of not.

The broadest reaching "here" about which I spoke with my interviewees was so-called Australia. To say Jews have a complicated relationship with Australia would be a supreme understatement; it is a heavy stream with competing undercurrents which clash with or amplify or fully neutralize each other. Australian–Jewish relations look like the very real possibility of the state of Israel being planned to take root in the Kimberleys [27]; the official prohibition of Jewish emigration under the White Australia Policy [28]; the blurred lines between anti-Zionism and antisemitism which work to simultaneously play down and high-pedestal Jewish experiences of both receiving and enacting oppression [29]; government surveillance of Jewish activists and "persons of interest" [30]; the collaboration between certain high-ranking Jewish politicians and the distinctly conservative[7] Liberal Party of Australia [31–33]; and the collective hypervigilance borne of direct attacks against Jewish places of worship and gathering which has resulted in armed guards and other high-end security measures being placed at many contemporary Australian synagogues [34, 35]. This is all without mentioning the highly organized and (originally)

---

7 Read: oppressive and openly hostile to marginalizsed peoples and lands.

bipartisan [36] Australian Zionist movement [37] which led to the development of things such as the Kimberley Project, and which has only gained momentum and power in more recent decades [38]. It is a mess.

There are no neat little boxes here. My interviewees were people who felt complexly about Jewish Australian life, who contended with these competing sociopolitical narratives which position Jews as a kind of pitiable-insidious-righteous-othered chimaera; a thoroughly self-confused animal that must constantly wrangle polarities, contradictions, and matters both nebulously abstract and existential in the most real sense. However, as this book slowly reveals,

Elsa: I was probably more conscious of the ways that I was being excluded from mainstream Christian and Anglo Australia rather than the Jewish community.

there is a core to which queer and trans Jews in particular cluster around, are drawn to. It is a disservice to speak of Jewish people in Australia in simplicities, as it is of any group which experiences societal othering or marginalization. Instead, I believe it is important to simply allow all the parts to exist, to touch or release from one another as necessary, and to tell a story that must be understood as interweaving parts – dragonscales both firmly and individually rooted yet perpetually undulating and causing friction in their inevitable overlapping. It is this overlap, this *swirling* discussed in the previous chapter, which forms this firm-yet-involute foundation of queer, trans, and Jewish experiences in so-called Australia.

To many of my interviewees, there was an undeniable sense of pride in their connection to Australia, an understanding of Jewish people as inseparable aspects of Australian culture and history. To others, living in Australia meant a constant awareness that one is living on unceded Aboriginal lands, that our citizenship in this country is facilitated by colonial mechanisms that subjugate others, for example, Blak people, flavour-of-the-month "unwanted" migrant

Liv: I work in wine

Shosh: Oh amazing. What do you mean by when you say work in wine?

Liv: I sell wine [. . .] through my family, actually. [. . .] My dad did an interview a couple of years ago [alongside other] founding families who started vineyards in Margaret River. And there's actually a whole set of Jews who are a part of it, which was really awesome. [. . .] For some reason, they just got really into making wine. But it was a lot of Eastern European families who moved over where they had limited trades. But [. . .] when you had a farm, then you had to work with the land. And that was a big thing. [. . .] It's a nice little diverse view of what Australia is. They were able to kind of leave that amazing imprint [. . .]. Now, when people think of Western Australia, we're known for our wine, and that's actually kind of thanks to the Jewish immigrants who came.

populations, refugees, and asylum seekers. Through my interviews it became clear that in fact, there was much more overlap than distinction amongst my interviewees between those two understandings; there was always an unease in navigating conversations around nationalism, citizenship, and occupation. Regardless of affiliation around Judaism, Zionism, and so on, my conversations found themselves circling time and time again towards experiences of isolation in many different (and at times opposing) social spheres. Israel/Palestine in particular felt almost like a spectre haunting many people's interactions, bordering on taboo, acting as a hard barrier to closeness, intimacy, and community.

Elite: Being Jewish [. . .] especially in these political times, is not necessarily something I like to scream from the rafters either. Because there's so many people [. . .] from the far left that, especially if you're Israeli, think that [. . .] you're a bit of a bad person.

This is something that absolutely resonates for me: even in writing what I have so far, I have felt this sense of dread. As a Jew, particularly one who has immigrated here to avoid conscription to the IDF, criticizing my new country of citizenship feels like spiting fate, or ignoring history. My existence here will never cease to feel dicey, citizenship a decreasingly reassuring marker of safety. As an anti-Zionist, particularly one with an Israeli birth certificate, criticizing Israeli apartheid has become a vital but incredibly daunting responsibility. It is one of my most obvious experiences of having sat on the wrong side of this situation, and I am dutiful in countering that impact. However, I have already forfeited every family connection I have in order to wrench myself from the IDF death machine, and I won't be making any friends with this book either. The sense of isolation is palpable to me, in this moment.

Elsa: I kind of associate different stages in my life as unpacking different intersections and parts of my identity. And I think when I was really young, like the part of my identity that I felt I really had to work through was being really short. I was like, "oh, man, I'm so short. Like, everyone makes fun". Like that was my thing. And then when I was a teenager, suddenly it was gender and how being a woman impacted me in the world. And then later it was being a Person of Colour or being Jewish. And I think probably one of the most recent ones has been being mixed race and how that has impacted my experiences.

I remember arriving to permanently live in Australia on September 10, 2001, at the age of 13, having already had multiple conversations with my mother about where it's ok to mention that we're Israeli (very few places) and where it's ok to speak Hebrew (at home, quietly in public). Of course, the very next day changed things for the worse: suddenly, any association with the Middle East became necrotic, and the entire region had become enmeshed in the Australian imaginary into one hostile place. My introduction to Australia was therefore one of secrecy, of navigating every single aspect of my identity in the narrowest and most careful way possible, with a laser focus on my Jewishness and place of origin. I was lucky; my relatively fluent English and thick American accent[8] meant most people read me, at least initially, as a Yank[9]. I must say that this is where my luck ended: I was broad, a head taller than my cohort, "ambiguously ethnic" to say the least, and hopeless in concealing my neurodivergence and queerness. The latter came into play the most; it was almost too much for the average Aussie schoolboy to process all of me, and quickly it seemed that "faggot"[10] would have to suffice as a catch-all descriptor. But I knew that term carried with it layers, even as a teen; I knew it stood for "different", "monstrous", "disgusting", "incomprehensible"... all things which equally apply to my Jewishness, to my birthplace, to the ways my bodymind differed in small or big ways from the bland-yet-vicious sea I found myself awash in. This isolation, this multi-prong rejection of oneself by others, is something that has never truly gone away for me, nor will it ever. In a sense, you could argue I was awakened to the intersections I'm exploring in this book very early in my life, and much of it was due to my forceful encounter with Australian culture.

Here: Jewish Community

If I were to summarize the experiences both myself and my participants have had with Jewish communities, it would be what José Esteban Muñoz [39] terms *disidentification*. Disidentification is neither a polarized nor a middle space; it is a movement towards and away from stereotypes, truths, and shadow aspects of one's identity, whether it is a queer or Jewish or another kind of identity. There was always a critical edge, a point of contention, even to those interviewees who considered themselves settled within their communities. Perhaps a joke will help here:

> A Jewish man has been stranded on a deserted island. Days turn to weeks turn to months turn to years, but eventually a rescue mission finds him alive and well. As they make their way to the shore, the man says: *Baruch HaShem, it is so good to see*

---

8 Courtesy of all the Jewish American settlers who had moved to Israel to become English teachers in the new US colony.

9 This was the slur of choice for me throughout my Australian schooling experience.

10 The other slur of choice.

you! I have survived remarkably well all by my lonesome here, would you like a tour of the island before we depart? The rescue workers agree, and the man begins his tour. *This is my hut, and my little vegetable garden, and this is the synagogue...* he says as he walks around gesturing at his various creations. *This is my exercise equipment, and my fishing gear, and this is the other synagogue...* At this point the rescue workers stop him, and ask: *why did you build two synagogues?* To which the man replies: *well, the first one I go to every day, and the other one I wouldn't set a fucking foot in!*

> *Shosh:* What does your sort of connection to Judaism look like for you?
>
> *Ariel:* Some days it feels like, it looks like, obligation.

The gag is as old as time itself, but the message is clear. We are brought back to Rojtman's [40] quote at the head of the previous chapter, to this notion that we are at once building Jewishness and bucking against it, always *swirling* between *what can be done, what must be done,* and *what has been done.* There is a balancing act between growth, obligation, and tradition, with the former constantly upheaving one's connection to the others, or the latter two suppressing one's access to the former. But they are not only separate entities; one might, for example, experience political motivation or personal ecstasy by harnessing oneself to certain Jewish obligations (e.g. Mitzvahs). Alternatively, there are many aspects of tradition and history which, when viewed through the right lens, are liberatory and exploratory rather than didactic in their relationship to customs and practices. Regardless, there is a fervent and constant push-and-pull between Jews living now and the legacy bestowed upon us.

> *Jonathan:*
> In the more Orthodox spaces [...] it's not specifically about my experiences with gender and sexuality, it's more about my own values as a person. I personally don't feel comfortable with highly gender-segregated spaces [...] where I feel like women are not valued as much as men. The times when I have been in Orthodox spaces, they felt very male-dominated [...].
> I feel more comfortable in more gender-egalitarian spaces. I don't feel particularly comfortable in gender segregated spaces. And that's just me as a man speaking, [...] I don't think it would be any different if I'd had different experiences with gender.

This is not just theory, it is very much praxis. Some of the arenas where this tension is engaged with are easily identifiable: gender, sexuality, race. My interviewees were not just navigating the pull between modernity and tradition in the abstract, in interpretation of texts and reimaginings of customs (though these did exist too, and will be discussed at length in a later chapter); they were wrangling with material ways in which traditions, institutions, and the Jewish people who are aligned with them often marginalized, minimized, or erased members of their own communities.

For some, these were personal experiences, whether they were encounters with homophobia, transphobia, racism, and/or sexism. For others, it was a matter of solidarity – with women, queers, trans people, Palestinians, and other Indigenous peoples.

No matter how my interviewees arrived at their positions, they were met with the conservative reality of many Jewish spaces. No matter the stream (e.g. Progressive, Orthodox), many Jewish spaces remain politically liberal at best, if not bordering on fundamentalist in certain (or many) aspects. Income, matrilineality, schooling, proximity to synagogue and Jewish communities, alongside the factors already mentioned above, all played a role in how "inside" or "outside" interviewees felt to the Jewish community. Returning to the notion of *disidentification*, it was truly fascinating to see the many ways my interviewees negotiated their points of difference from the social narratives and expectations within their Jewish families, friendship groups, and broader communities. Some outcomes were to be expected: many people had no active engagement with, or sometimes even a desire to engage with, established Jewish communities

> *Slam:* I [. . .] have always rejected [religion] because of [. . .] the dryness of synagogue, and of school. [. . .] I went to the Jewish school [and] it's kind of [. . .] one big pocket. It's like one big loaf of bread that is the racism and the anti-Islamic shit and the synagogue and the transphobia and [. . .] you know being arty instead of a doctor. Like all of that shit is in that one loaf of bread [. . .] that I've rejected. So I rejected going to the synagogue before I knew I was trans. [. . .] I have thought about going to synagogue since [. . .] coming out as trans and knowing myself, but it seems too tricky. So I just stopped.

and institutions. Yet, even for those most removed, there remained a spark of connection, an in-depth understanding of, or curiosity about, Jewishness that existed outside of *what must be done*. Others found little or no personal/religious connection to Jewishness or even G-d more broadly but nonetheless found the connective elements of Jewish traditions to form a vital aspect of their life. In all cases, there was a sense of proximity to community, even if that proximity waxed and waned, or manifested through unorthodox channels.

I have personally found myself in the former category; although I was raised around Jewish traditions, my move to Australia also marked the end of my engagement with Holy Days and practices for over a decade. It wasn't until my mid-20s, in the slowly bubbling eruption that

> *Maddy:* There are shared experiences that I haven't had that I feel people characterize as Jewishness, things like going to the Jewish school growing up, going to shul. Like having a Bat Mitzvah, all that kind of stuff that I just haven't had.

was to become me coming to terms with my queerness, that I allowed myself to consider my relationship to G-d as I had been raised with. The main Jewish community in Perth was based on the opposite side of the city to where I grew up. My family had no connection to other Jews, certainly not on those terms anyway. I had no Jewish friends until my 20s, and knew less than a handful in the scenes I found myself around in my teens. All I had were faint memories and stereotypes intermixed with some broader spiritual understandings I'd gathered growing up in a very New Age environment.

Even today, I find myself scraggling for Jewish community. I have more Jewish friends now than I ever did before, partly due to my increased visibility as a Jew doing Jewish research. I'm much more engaged with the traditions than I have been in earlier years, though this too ebbs and flows depending on other life factors. But I would hesitate to term my experience as one of community, certainly in the ways I've heard it described both by some of my interviewees and other people (Jewish and non-Jewish) who I've spoken to about this topic. I experience an affinity, for sure, and a certain level of relatability, but my access to Jewish community in a real sense is mitigated by many factors both within and outside of Judaism[11].

Shosh: Do you feel like you sort of have to [. . .] switch how [. . .] you talk about this stuff?

Jamaica: Absolutely. [. . .] Whether it is a matter of the fact that I operate in a lot of different contexts as well [the fact that] I'm mixed race, I'm bisexual, I'm mixed faith, so I code switch a lot. And that's something I'm very used to. So depending on how someone else positions themself, I will often position myself in a way that I think they will understand

It would be disingenuous, and counter to some of the arguments made earlier in this book, to lay responsibility for any experiences of exclusion or community detachment squarely with Jewishness itself. There are many external reasons why Australian Jewish communities work the way they do: the xenophobia and bigotry of Australian culture have most certainly forced Jewish communities to cluster and close ranks, to code switch [41], to privilege proximity to whiteness and wealth[12] in its membership in order to "blend", and to form close bonds with Israel as a means of keeping an international power close by.

Nonetheless, communities, even marginalized ones, cannot remain beholden to the narratives and practices foisted upon them, or else they risk ceasing to be distinct from the fast-advancing and ever-growing Blob [42] of assimilation [43]. We therefore need to hold ourselves and our own communities accountable,

---

11 Many of which I have already detailed elsewhere in this book.
12 And other forms of social privilege, e.g. heterosexuality and thinness.

to remain vigilant of the ways our own traditions and practices reflect settler-colonialism, white supremacy, heternormativity, cissexism, and so on.

This is not an argument for Jewish exceptionalism; many of our customs and traditions carry the vestigial tail of bygone eras which were inherently patriarchal and oppressive in nature [44], such as matrilineality as the only means of furthering the Jewish people [45]. But we must evolve, as we always have! You need not look any further than the relatively recent introduction of practices such as modern eruvim[13] [46, 47] and documents such as Aruch Hashulchan[14] [48], each less than 200 years old in their current manifestations, to understand the inherent responsivity and flexibility of Judaism. Certain streams, such as Conservative and Reform Judaism, have produced publications which explicate their points of divergence from canonical texts and practices, as a means of finding a balance between faith, tradition, and contemporary life [49, 50]. That alone provides an indication that when Jews are ready to enact change, we do so directly, intentionally, and meaningfully. Therefore we must ask the question: what is getting in the way of Australian Jewish communities changing into more politically inclusive and progressive spaces?

The undercurrents leading to exclusion exist down the same axis as other major religious and religion-affiliated groups: religious fundamentalism within Judaism tends to go hand-in-hand with political conservativism [51, 52]. This leads to the expected sociopolitical outcomes of these kinds of alignments; despite some reform and much resistance both within and outside these communities [53–57], religiously and politically conservative streams (e.g. Orthodoxy) remain largely opposed to gay rights and other equity and social justice movements [58], as well as to other peoples who may "deviate" from Halakha[15] [59, 60]. This means that queer and trans people (as well as others) who are engaged in these movements experience significant discrimination and exclusion, as well as the personal impact of that violence [61, 62].

> Justin: I think if you grew up or if you identify as Q[ueer] [...] you're going to have some kind of different lens in general [...] to varying degrees. [...] That's why [...] I don't like going to synagogue, and men and women sitting separately. I chat about this with my family, my parents, and you know it broadly [...] doesn't really bother them. It's just whatever they've always [...] known. They don't care to [...] challenge it in a huge way, [...] it doesn't bother them like it bugs me. And that has to come from being queer.

---

13 A physical parameter indicating the spaces Jews are allowed to travel within on Shabbat.
14 The canonization of previous texts on Jewish practices which detail the 613 Halakhic laws.
15 The set of rules governing "proper" Jewish religious conduct.

> *Madelaine:* I sort of stopped going to synagogue. My grandfather would go to an Orthodox synagogue and I'd sit upstairs and hate it. So I stopped going when I was a teenager.

Nevertheless, marginalized voices have always been present in these spaces, ensuring their opposition to the way Jewish institutions, leaders, and communities negate and suppress the diversity of Jewish peoples is heard loud and clear. Queer and trans Jewish activists have always played a role in shaping liberation and justice movements, and continue to do so to this day both in Australia and many other places around the world [63–68]. The call to recognize queer and trans Jews as "twice blessed" [69], as a group to be celebrated rather than denigrated, and who play a unique and transformative role within Jewish religio-cultural life [70] is slowly but surely being heeded. You need to look no further than the people interviewed for this book to understand the impact of queer and trans Jews on the world around them. Among my interviewees were medical professionals, artists, policymakers, activists, writers, parents, and academics[16] – roles which are most often oriented towards care, transformation, and growth.

I'm not interested in furthering a narrative of "contribution to society" as a tool for "earning one's place" in one's communities, and I don't believe it is necessary to be a triple threat[17] of some sort to earn your humanity and status. But it cannot be understated that many queer and trans (and other marginalized) Jews have no choice but to excel or professionalize, and to become advocates for social justice causes within their communities, simply due to the sheer opposing forces that exist within even the most "progressive" Jewish spaces. I've seen an entire so-called Progressive congregation pray for Israeli troops[18], and a Conservative Rabbi crack bigoted jokes at the bima[19] in such a matter-of-fact way that they nearly zoomed right past me; all without any opposition or exclamation from congregants or other leaders. As an invited guest[20], and someone who already stuck out like a sore thumb in both scenarios, I felt unable to comment. I had hoped someone else would step in, someone who was a member of that synagogue's community, someone with enough status and chutzpah and drive for justice to cut through the crap. Instead, the sermons proceeded without interruption, and I found myself using the only tool

16 Most ticked two or more of these boxes.
17 Academic, musician, and comedian in my case.
18 No mention of Palestinians, of course.
19 Synagogue pulpit.
20 Which I nearly always am.

accessible to me at the time: departure. It amazes me even now, as I reflect on these events, to consider the power of the crowd, the choices made by that crowd, and the sheer helplessness it left me with. These entrenched bigotries, this push to quieten personal politics for the sake of acquiescing to some notion of community connection, are something that affects many marginalized Jews and their allies. This leaves most of us with a burning and unanswerable question: how can you truly be "in community" if you cannot be yourself?

Here: Queer Community

While the term "queer community" serves as a convenient catch-all when discussing LGBTQIA+ rights, it also carries with it an implication of a kind of instantaneous identity-based membership which begs further questioning. Are you a member of the (or a) queer community simply by the fact of your queerness? How do we differentiate this collectivizing sense of a global or national queer community from the lived, daily, and relational experience of community? These are not new questions, and the answers seem to only further diversify and bifurcate the longer we continue our journey in understanding queerness as something that is not simply individual but also communal. Lisa Duggan [71], thirty years ago at the time of writing this, provides an exploration of the range of perspectives on the notion of a "queer community" from writers and activists across the United States. These range from queer community being an almost passive, expected, and natural outcome of queers living under oppressive circumstances; queer community as a kind of perpetually oxymoronic collectivization of those of us who are innately removed from collectivity by our sexuality and gender; through to a refusal of any inherent collectivity based solely on sexuality or gender, and a vision of queer community as an action-based coalition of people seeking justice and liberation for all. In short, queer community either exists through mere individual sexualities and genders, an oscillation between rejection and acceptance by both the general public and other queers, or as an intentional political practice which cannot hinge on identity alone. Or all of the above.

Similar considerations and differing or alternating perspectives came through from my interviewees' experiences. Many expressed feeling a sense of queer community in their life by their mere co-existence alongside other queer people;

Hunter: A significant number of people in my [university] year are out as gay [. . .]. I think I'm the only trans person, but the queer community is much more open and that changes your relationship with it.

there seems to be a kind of power in simply knowing that others share those experiences of sexuality and gender and that there are ways to exist queerly in the world that are not entirely subject to the callousness and rejection spitooned at us from cisheterosexual society. Although "outness" and mere visibility are something I have heavily criticized in previous writing [72], there is no use downplaying the role that other people living queerly play in a person's life simply by that person's knowledge of their existence. This is particularly true for those who, for whatever reason, find themselves within largely or entirely cishet social circles and surroundings, whether due to their profession, the particular makeup of the other types of communities they belong to, or for any other reasons.

It's an ongoing joke among queer folk that we make the world a little gayer just by walking down the street, and I would argue this is something that I have experienced from both sides of the story. I never had a moment where I saw a visible queer celebrity[21] and thought "that's me!", partly because my experience of gender and sexuality runs down a particularly convoluted path[22]. But I have spent most of my life around queers and freaks (the distinctions become less relevant the older I get), and their divergence from the beaten path of heterosexual and cisgender behaviours, aesthetics, and mindsets will forever stick in my mind. I have a very fond memory of an older, somewhat out queer friend wearing their leather jacket to every punk show sporting a full-scale illustration of two men jerking each other off and going across the entire back half, which they did to "piss straight dudes off". Nearly two decades have passed since we met, but that bold and vulgar fuck-you to the deeply straight-dominated punk scene we were both in instilled some very important lessons about how to engage with, refuse, and arguably karate homophobia using its own force. This is not to say my friend, and others like him, didn't suffer consequences for these flagrant displays of faggotry, quite the opposite; no doubt most if not all had some chipped teeth and interesting scars to show for their efforts. But those too became a symbol of perseverance for me, something to aspire to beyond the often performative and heavily co-opted "broken homes and broken bones" [73] attitude that is so synonymous with (straight) punk music and culture. Finally, something *meaningful* to have broken bones over beyond macho mosh pit posturing!

However, this is distinctly *not* a description of community; I continued to be alone in my queerness, the topic being largely absent from discussions

---

21 Which were in short supply then.
22 My gender and sexuality bingo card is nearly full.

with the exception of the occasional "friendly" homophobic jab from one of my supposed compatriots. Merely knowing others around me were "adjacent" to queerness in one way or another was not enough, and I found myself sorely longing for deep and open conversations, for friendships and intimate relationships where my queerness was not experienced as a disruption but as a cherished aspect of my personhood, for places where I could "fit in" without sucking in my stomach and minimizing myself. Eventually,

Dahni: Belonging in terms of the LGBTI community... for me that's been very much about finding [. . .] my people within that. [. . .] For [. . .] quite a few years now, most of my friends are lesbians, which is not how it [. . .] was for a large part of my life. And for me I think that's because [. . .] that's where I [. . .] feel that I belong.

this led me to explore the few queer spaces available to me around the time of my "coming out", namely the gay pub and gay club which had managed to weather Perth's distinctly anti-gay culture and its impact on open gay culture. I also found myself in more queer spaces when my punk bands would tour, most notably in Naarm/Melbourne[23]. For a community-starved queer from the most isolated city in the country, these places felt like beacons, drawing me towards them and warmly illuminating what otherwise felt like an austere way of life. Despite the persistence of anti-queer sentiments in Australian culture both historically and contemporarily [74, 75], I could find enough morsels of love, connection, and mirrored experiences to satisfy my lonely queer soul.

As I continue to move through different queer communities, it is impossible to ignore the ways in which communities expand and contract depending on the actions and makeup of local people and groups. One perspective on the implications of in/action on community is Robert Reynolds' "What Happened to Gay Life?" [76], which posits that Sydney's gay scene has experienced a notable downturn in the 2000s, as a result of collective disengagement from radical politics and a sharp turn towards appeasing the mainstream. Reynolds concludes the book on a rather negative note, with the future of gay life in Sydney seemingly shrouded in uncertainty and threatened by a further downward trajectory. Although the book is rather narrow in its scope,

Madelaine: I started this lesbian Book Club, which is still going, and I found that really helpful just to be around, just once a month, [. . .] other queer women. And I'm a nerd so I'll read a book, but also [to] be around those queers and feel connected, and feel like "oh okay, I might be this in really heteronormative space all week and be somewhere I don't feel quite comfortable with, but at least I have a reprieve".

23 My first Sydney experience was light on the queers, heavy on the Nazi skinheads.

focusing on interviews with (cisgender) gay men, its implications are clear: a community is only as strong and vivid as the people contributing to it. This perspective reflects both what Duggan's earlier work describes and some of the ways my interviewees discussed their connection to a queer community, insofar as community connectivity is not simply a passive acknowledgement of the existence of others but rather something which can (and perhaps should) be formed and maintained through collectivization.

> *Natan:* It felt more accepting to shift away from Jewish community to the queer community. It's just more exciting. Like I really like to party.

There is also a notable shift in moving from Jewish community spaces to queer ones. While Jewish communal life continues to encircle around the (cisheteronormative) synagogue, despite increasing movement to the contrary [77], queer community has always situated itself in clubs, galleries, and public bathrooms – venues which are geared towards ecstasy, unification, and exploration, even if often done in secret or hidden deep within an otherwise heterosexual context [78–80]. This is not to say that Jewishness is inherently lacking in ecstasy, either within or outside the synagogue [81], but rather that the ways in which physical meeting places have evolved tend to diverge heavily between queer and Jewish spaces. While it's true that Jews have had to practise in secret for centuries, including setting up "crypto-Jewish synagogues" [82], the position of synagogues in contemporary society is one which is both visible and socially sanctioned, at least in part, by the broader communities or nation-states they exist within. Meanwhile, though queers have always found ways to socialize and bond, even through a global pandemic [83, 84], queer life continues to be affected by a decline in gaybourhoods and brick-and-mortar public establishments, and the increasing emergence of alternative forms of relating that either (temporarily) nestle themselves within or entirely sidestep normative architectural and societal structures [85–87].

The difference between well-funded and security-staffed synagogues and the existence of a handful of openly and intentionally queer-oriented pubs and clubs even in the most progressive cities in the world is stark, and carries implications for participation in community for those wanting to engage with either or both groups. It's worth acknowledging that the establishments that exist for both groups have issues of exclusion which run along familiar axes, such as inaccessibility and white dominance. However, the need to access queer community is often facilitated exactly by the negation of the terms of engagement which facilitate access to the Jewish community; that is to say, Jewish community engagement tends to hinge on biological family connection and supposedly clear-cut ties to tradition and lineage, whereas access to queer community often occurs as a direct result of the violation of those connections. Similarly, Jews who have ambiguous family histories, who do not have blood relatives within their local synagogue or community, or whose lives and personhoods exist in contradiction to the politics of these institutions and groups (read: being queer or trans) may be much more likely to seek out communities outside of Jewishness. This is true even outside the realm of the intersections of Judaism and gender/sexuality; you need to look no further than phenomena such as the JewBu (Jewish Buddhist) [88] or the sheer magnitude of Jews joining cults such as the Rajneeshees[24] [89] to understand both Jews' deep drive for belonging and the ways Jewish disidentification may ultimately lead to complete disconnection from Jewish faith and culture.

Although many of my interviewees expressed a sense of belonging within queer spaces, it is important to note that some did not feel very connected to their local queer communities, or any queer communities at all. For some, it was a matter of chance, the result of simply not finding a foothold in a community or not viewing queerness as a vital hinging point for friendships and relating. The latter is a particularly interesting factor, one that seems to indicate different worldviews for different interviewees. Being queer and trans can feel all-encompassing, and become a core aspect of a person's identity which sits at the fore of their relationships to others. But that is not the case for all people, much the same as any other aspect of one's life or identity. Gender and sexuality may just be a fact of life for some, rather than their entire interpretative lens, in the same way that disability or race can be situated as either forefront sociopolitical identifiers or simply factors which affect one's life. While this can mean a disconnection from, or perhaps even disinterest in, queer community participation, it does not leave people high and

Jonathan: I definitely don't feel a sense of belonging among the LGBT community most of the time. I usually feel quite alienated at LGBT events.

Shosh: How come?

Jonathan: I don't really know. [. . .] I've never really connected. I think partly [. . .] gender and sexuality, [. . .] it's never felt like the thing that I wanted people to connect with me about. I've never wanted that to be the thing that I had big conversations with people about. I would much rather talk to people about religion or books or music or, you know, a whole host of other things than gender or sexuality for the most part.

---

24 A group to which myself and several members of my family have belonged to at one point or another.

dry. Community belonging is complex (as will be discussed in a later chapter), and we each form ours differently.

Elsa: For me [. . .] the most jarring factor in the queer community is people will post a status or something warning people about [. . .] Nazi actions or like a swastika somewhere or something. But completely omit Jews from that narrative. And they're saying like "queers and People of Colour, [. . .] look out today, this is going on" and it's like, did you forget about Jews? Because that was really us. Like, we were really at the centre of that. We just get omitted a lot from that narrative. And I think that that is maybe the most hurtful thing, seeing people who are so politically engaged push Jewishness and the political issues that surround the oppression of Jewish people [. . .] completely [. . .] out of the narrative.

For other interviewees, however, their sense of disconnection from community came as a direct result of their Jewishness. It would have been disingenuous to simply describe the queer community experience as one where outcasts are accepted wholesale, difference being the only criteria for entry. Australian queer communities still exist within broader Australian culture and discourse, which remain bigoted, and specifically anti-Semitic [90], at a fundamental level [91–93]. Despite the immense solidarity work done by queer Jews across both Jewish and queer communities (including work done by some of my interviewees), there remains a sense of othering when engaging with Australian queer communities as visibly Jewish queers. Whether it is a default assumption about one's relationship to the Israeli occupation of Palestine, underlying stereotypes about Jews, or even something as simple as running so-called "Jewish" queer events on Shabbat or another Holy Day which restricts one's capacity to attend, a sense of disconnection from (mostly white Anglo) queer spaces is practically inevitable.

Justin: Did I have some sort of vague experiences with queer people and anti-Semitism? Yes. [But] I don't remember them specifically. It's just a sense.

However, as with many experiences of discrimination, it is often less a matter of direct violence or outright statements of anti-Semitic rejection and more a subtle, cumulative process which colours the landscape. Homophobia does not always manifest as gay bashing or the Grim Reaper campaign [94] but often in illusive and implicit aspects of how queers and trans peoples are related to by heterosexuals and cisgender people. The same goes for experiences of antisemitism; one does not need to see news about yet another synagogue attack or hear the same boring questions about sex through a hole in the sheet [95] to experience an affect of othering when engaging with the non-Jewish world. This subtle affective atmosphere permeates all interactions within an anti-Semitic society, including queer communities. It often manifests itself in absence rather than presence: the absence of openly Jewish speakers at events; the absence of recognition of Jews' contribution to queer history (with few exceptions, e.g. Les Feinberg); and most notably the absence of conversation around the positive aspects of Judaism in relation to queerness. This latter absence is often presented as an avoidance of inducing "Judeo-Christian" religious trauma, the term itself being both a paradox and a means of erasing Judaism's distinctiveness from the oppression of Christianity and its subsects. Yes, there are many queers who have been negatively affected by their religious Jewish upbringing, but to reduce Jewishness to just another restrictive and fundamentalist religion is to deny the incredible changes our peoples have brought forth both within secular and religious aspects of our collective existences.

Conclusion

There is no easy way to sum up queer Jews' experiences of communities within so-called Australia. We exist at a crucible of ethnicity, religion, gender, sexuality, and other facets of life which intersect and often come into conflict with the spaces and communities we find ourselves in. As I will discuss in the final chapter of this book, these experiences of community can have deeper, more intrapersonal implications on how we envision and experience belonging more broadly. Queer Jewish experiences of communities run the gamut, from satisfaction and connection through to displeasure and rejection, and every combination of elements within and between those polarities. It is impossible to deny the role that societal discourse plays in affecting our experiences of different communal spaces, and the implications of the sociohistorical role of both queerness and Jewishness within the Australian social imaginary. Queer Jews thus find themselves pulled to different ends, towards different communities and ways of engaging, towards widely varying desires around community, solidarity, and personal expression. It is this latter point which will be the focus of the next chapter.

References

[1] Gee G, Dudgeon P, Schultz C, et al. Aboriginal and Torres Strait Islander social and emotional wellbeing. *Work Together Aborig Torres Strait Isl Ment Health Wellbeing Princ Pract* 2014; 2: 55–68.

[2] Strelein L. From mabo to yorta yorta: native title law in Australia. *Wash UJL Pol* 2005; 19: 225.

[3] Whyte K. Indigenous climate change studies : Indigenizing futures, decolonizing the Anthropocene. *Engl Lang Notes* 2017; 55: 153–162.

[4] Warlenius R. Decolonizing the atmosphere: The Climate Justice Movement on climate debt. *J Environ Dev* 2018; 27: 131–155.

[5] Potter E. Contesting imaginaries in the Australian city: Urban planning, public storytelling and the implications for climate change. *Urban Stud* 2020; 57: 1536–1552.

[6] Nash D, Memmott P, Reser J, et al. We're the same as the Inuit!: Exploring Australian Aboriginal perceptions of climate change in a multidisciplinary mixed methods study. *Energy Res Soc Sci* 2018; 45: 107–119.

[7] Kellerman A. *Society and Settlement: Jewish Land of Israel in the Twentieth Century.* SUNY Press, 2012.

[8] Malabou C, Miller S. *The New Wounded: From Neurosis to Brain Damage.* US, United States: Fordham University Press, <http://ebookcentral.proquest.com/lib/curtin/detail.act ion?docID=3239638> (2012, accessed 26 April 2021).

[9] Sand S. *The Invention of the Land of Israel: From Holy Land to Homeland.* Verso Books, 2012.

[10] Malabou C. *The Ontology of the Accident: An Essay on Destructive Plasticity.* Wiley, 2012.

[11] Walsh SD, Tuval-Mashiach R. Ethiopian emerging adult immigrants in Israel: Coping with discrimination and racism. *Youth Soc* 2012; 44: 49–75.

[12] Furberg Moe MC. *Peripheral Nationhood: Being Israeli in Kiryat Shemona.* Phd, The London School of Economics and Political Science (LSE), <http://ethe ses.lse.ac.uk/449/> (2012, accessed 26 April 2021).

[13] Schulman S. *Israel/Palestine and the Queer International.* Duke University Press, 2012.

[14] Kristal T. Slicing the Pie: State policy, class organization, class integration, and Labor's share of Israeli national income. *Soc Probl* 2013; 60: 100–127.

[15] Ahluwalia P. Fanon's nausea: The hegemony of the white nation. *Soc Identities* 2003; 9: 341–356.

[16] Veracini L. The other shift: Settler colonialism, Israel, and the occupation. *J Palest Stud* 2013; 42: 26–42.

[17] Gechtman R. Jews and non-territorial autonomy: Political programmes and historical perspectives. *Ethnopolitics* 2016; 15: 66–88.

[18] Alroey G. "Zionism without Zion"? Territorialist ideology and the Zionist Movement, 1882–1956. *Jew Soc Stud* 2011; 18: 1–32.

[19] Brager J. *Doykeit.* JB Brager, 2012.

[20] Kijek K. Max Weinreich, assimilation and the social politics of Jewish nation-building. *East Eur Jew Aff* 2011; 41: 25–55.

[21] Boyarin D. *The No-State Solution: A Jewish Manifesto.* Yale University Press, 2023.

[22] Neusner J. *Zionism and "The Jewish Problem",* 2020; Routledge.

[23] Berdugo L. *The Weaponized Camera in the Middle East: Videography, Aesthetics, and Politics in Israel and Palestine.* Bloomsbury Publishing, 2021.

[24] Cohen M. Wall and tower: *Netw Knowl J MeCCSA Postgrad Netw* 2019; 12: 20–35.

[25] Avineri S. *The Making of Modern Zionism: The Intellectual Origins of the Jewish State.* Hachette UK, 2017.

[26] Williams DM. Contemporary anarchist and anarchistic movements. *Sociol Compass* 2018; 12: e12582.

[27] Rutland SD. *The Jews in Australia.* Cambridge University Press, 2006.

[28] Gouttman R. A Jew, and coloured too! Immigration of "Jews of middle east origin" to Australia, 1949–58. *Immigr Minor* 1993; 12: 75–91.

[29] Mendes P. Denying the Jewish experience of oppression: Australian Jews against Zionism and Anti-Semitism (JAZA) and the 3CR controversy1. *History* 2011; 45: 499–500.

[30] Komesaroff M. The Jewish left, Asio and my family. *Aust Jew Hist Soc J* 2020; 24.

[31] van Onselen P. What's right?: The future of the Liberal Party. *Monthly, The,* <https://sea rch-infor mit-org.dbgw.lis.cur tin.edu.au/doi/abs/10.3316/iel apa.9882 5651 0740 771> (2011, accessed 29 April 2021).

[32] Gauja A. The "Push" for primaries: What drives party organisational reform in Australia and the United Kingdom? *Aust J Polit Sci* 2012; 47: 641–658.

[33] Courtice B. Meet the "minister against renewables". *Green Left Wkly* 2017; 7.

[34] Rutland S. 2. Negotiating religious dialogue: A response to the recent increase of anti-Semitism in Australia. *Negot Sacred* 2006; 17.

[35] Goldberg D. Guards at every shule: Pittsburgh highlights a sad Australian reality. +61J, <https://plus61j.net.au/plus61j-voices/guards-every-shule-pittsburgh-highlights-sad-austral ian-reality/> (2018, accessed 29 April 2021).

[36] Mendes P. The Australian Left's support for the creation of the state of Israel, 1947–48. *Labour Hist* 2009; 97: 137–148.

[37] Crown AD. The initiatives and influences in the development of Australian Zionism, 1850–1948. *Jew Soc Stud* 1977; 39: 299–322.

[38] Bloch B. Unsettling Zionism: Diasporic consciousness and Australian Jewish identities, <https://res earc hdir ect.wester nsyd ney.edu.au/island ora/obj ect/uws%3A2 532/> (2005, accessed 29 April 2021).

[39] Muñoz JE. *Disidentifications: Queers of Color and the Performance of Politics.* U of Minnesota Press, 2013.

[40] Rojtman B. *Black Fire on White Fire: An Essay on Jewish Hermeneutics, from Midrash to Kabbalah.* Univ of California Press, 1998.

[41] Heller M, Wei L. Code-switching and the politics of language. In: *The Bilingualism Reader.* Routledge, pp. 163–176.

[42] The Blob. *Horror, Sci-Fi, Tonylyn Productions Inc., Valley Forge Films,* Fairview Productions, 1958.

[43] Fishberg M. *Jews, Race, and Environment.* Routledge, 2017.

[44] Ross T. *Expanding the Palace of Torah: Orthodoxy and Feminism.* UPNE, 2004.

[45] Cohen SJD. The origins of the Matrilineal Principle in Rabbinic Law. *AJS Rev* 1985; 10: 19–53.

[46] Rapoport M. Creating place, creating community: The intangible boundaries of the Jewish "Eruv". *Environ Plan Soc Space* 2011; 29: 891–904.

[47] Mintz A. *Halakhah in America: The History of City Eruvin, 1894–1962.* New York University, 2011.

[48] Rosen M. The interaction of Kabbalah and Halachah in the Aruch ha-Shulchan. *Internet Publ Httpwww Maqom Comjournalpaper22 Pdf.*

[49] Dorff EN. *Modern Conservative Judaism: Evolving Thought and Practice.* U of Nebraska Press, 2018.

[50] Tobias P, Keren-Black J. *A Judaism for the Twenty-First Century.* Createspace Independent Pub, 2010.

[51] Haji R, Lalonde RN, Durbin A, et al. A multidimensional approach to identity: Religious and cultural identity in young Jewish Canadians. *Group Process Intergroup Relat* 2011; 14: 3–18.

[52] Stadler N. Ethnography of exclusion: Initiating a dialogue with fundamentalist men. *Nashim J Jew Womens Stud Gend Issues* 2007; 14: 185–208.

[53] Stadler N. *Yeshiva Fundamentalism: Piety, Gender, and Resistance in the Ultra-Orthodox World.* NYU Press, 2009.

[54] Gleibman S. The Jewish Queer Continuum in Yeshiva Narratives. *Shofar Interdiscip J Jew Stud* 2017; 35: 1–31.

[55] Rapoport C. *Judaism and Homosexuality: An Authentic Orthodox View.* 2004 [Doctoral thesis, Georgetown University]

[56] Trans Torah. Trans Torah. *Trans Torah,* <http://transtorah.org> (2018).

[57] Congregation Sha'ar Zahav. *Siddur Shaar Zahav: The All-Inclusive Siddur.* Congregation Sha'ar Zahav, 2009.

[58] Lazar A, Hammer JH. Religiousness and anti-gay/lesbian attitudes: The mediating function of intratextual religious fundamentalism. *Psychol Violence* 2018; 8: 763.

[59] Rosenthal RS. Of pearls and fish: An analysis of Jewish legal texts on sexuality and their significance for contemporary American Jewish movements. *Colum J Gend L* 2006; 15: 485.

[60] Shahak I, Mezvinsky N. *Jewish Fundamentalism in Israel.* Pluto Press London, 1999.

[61] Brody KD, Sperber D. *Mourning and Celebration: Jewish, Orthodox and Gay, Past & Present.* Transcréation, 2009.

[62] Shilo G, Antebi N, Mor Z. Individual and community resilience factors among lesbian, gay, bisexual, queer and questioning youth and adults in Israel. *Am J Community Psychol* 2015; 55: 215–227.

[63] Hartal G. Becoming periphery – Israeli LGBT "Peripheralization". *ACME Int J Crit Geogr* 2015; 14: 571–597.

[64] Avishai O. Religious queer people beyond identity conflict: Lessons from orthodox LGBT Jews in Israel. *J Sci Study Relig* 2020; 59: 360–378.

[65] Willett G, Brickell C. LGBT activism in Australia and New Zealand. In: *The Wiley Blackwell Encyclopedia of Gender and Sexuality Studies.* American Cancer Society, pp. 1–5.

[66] Kochberg S, Knan S, Hackett R. Rainbow Jews: Now & Then, Parts I and II: Australian radio broadcast programmes on pioneer LGBT+ UK Jews from the 1960s onwards.

[67] Lesh J. Twentieth-century Jewish LGBTQ London and the Rainbow Jews Heritage Project. *Change Time* 2018; 8: 206–225.

[68] Feinberg L. *Transgender Liberation: A Movement Whose Time Has Come*. World View Forum, 1992.

[69] Balka C, Rose A. *Twice Blessed: On Being Lesbian, Gay, and Jewish*. Beacon Press, 1989.

[70] Moon D. Beyond the dichotomy: Six religious views of homosexuality. *J Homosex* 2014; 61: 1215–1241.

[71] Duggan L. Making it perfectly queer. *Social Rev* 1992; 22: 11.

[72] Rosenberg S. Coming in: Queer narratives of sexual self-discovery. *J Homosex* 2018; 65: 1788–1816.

[73] Rancid. Nihilism. *Epitaph*, 1994.

[74] Robinson S. *Homophobia: An Australian History*. Federation Press, 2008.

[75] Willett G. The darkest decade: Homophobia in 1950s Australia. *Aust Hist Stud* 1997; 27: 120–132.

[76] Reynolds R. *What Happened to Gay Life?* University of New South Wales Press, <https://rese arch ers.mq.edu.au/en/publi cati ons/what-happe ned-to-gay-life> (2007, accessed 29 July 2021).

[77] Judaism Unbound, Gross RB. The Deli Is My Synagogue, <https://www.judaismunbound.com/podcast/episode-278-rachel-gross> (accessed 29 July 2021).

[78] Desroches FJ. Tearoom trade: A research update. *Qual Sociol* 1990; 13: 39–61.

[79] Buckland F. *Impossible Dance: Club Culture and Queer World-Making*. Wesleyan University Press, 2002.

[80] Browne K, Bakshi L. We are here to party? Lesbian, gay, bisexual and trans leisurescapes beyond commercial gay scenes. *Leis Stud* 2011; 30: 179–196.

[81] Wolfson ER. Yeridah la-Merkavah: Typology of ecstasy and enthronement in ancient Jewish mysticism. *Mystics Book Themes Top Typol* 1993; 13–44.

[82] Dutton CJ. *The Road To Return: The First Crypto-Jewish Synagogue*. University of Southern California, 2007.

[83] Trott B. Queer Berlin and the Covid-19 crisis: A politics of contact and ethics of care. *Interface J Soc Mov* 2020; 12: 88–108.

[84] Anderson AR, Knee E. Queer isolation or queering isolation? Reflecting upon the ramifications of COVID-19 on the future of queer leisure spaces. *Leis Sci* 2021; 43: 118–124.

[85] Miles S. Let's (not) go outside: Grindr, hybrid space, and digital queer neighborhoods. *Life Afterlife Gay Neighborhoods* 2021; 203.

[86] Coffin J. Plateaus and afterglows: Theorizing the afterlives of gayborhoods as post-places. *Life Afterlife Gay Neighborhoods* 2021; 371.

[87] Miles S, Coffin J, Ghaziani A, et al. After/lives: Insights from the COVID-19 pandemic for gay neighborhoods. *Life Afterlife Gay Neighborhoods Renaiss Resurgence* 2021; 393–418.

[88] Sigalow E. *American JewBu: Jews, Buddhists, and Religious Change*. Princeton University Press, 2019.

[89] Latkin CA, Hagan RA, Littman RA, et al. Who lives in utopia? A brief report on the Rajneeshpuram research project. *SA Sociol Anal* 1987; 73–81.

[90] Goldflam A. Queerer than Queer. *J Homosex* 1999; 36: 135–142.

[91] Hill B, Dodd J, Uink B, et al. Pride, belonging and community: What does this mean if you are Aboriginal and LGBT+ and living in Western Australia? *J Sociol* 2022; 14407833221093402.

[92] Riggs DW. Anti-Asian sentiment amongst a sample of white Australian men on gaydar. *Sex Roles* 2013; 68: 768–778.

[93] Riggs DW. Gaps, questions, and resistance. *Psych Life Racism Gay Mens Communities* 2017; 137.

[94] Morlet A, Guinan JJ, Diefenthaler I, et al. The impact of the "grim reaper" national AIDS educational campaign on the Albion Street (AIDS) Centre and the AIDS Hotline. *Med J Aust* 1988; 148: 282–287.

[95] Ribner DS, Kleinplatz PJ. The hole in the sheet and other myths about sexuality and Judaism. *Sex Relatsh Ther* 2007; 22: 445–456.

[96] Foucault M. *Les aveux de la chair*. Gallimard, 2018.

· 3 ·

FAMILIES, INNER WORLDS, AND QUEERNESS

While queerness and Jewishness are immutably intermingled with community experiences, and have consequences for how one navigates particular environments, groups, and societies, the seed of these experiences rests within one's inner life. These inner lives are shaped by our core inner worlds [1], our families [2], and our personal interpretations of life events and societal narratives writ large [3, 4]. All these factors contribute to the formation of what you might call identity, or the self, though the roles, values, and weights of each factor vary from person to person and from day to day. This is particularly true of both Jews and queer peoples (and queer Jewish peoples), whose experiences within these most personal contexts can be highly impactful on the ways we then proceed to navigate our lives. Whether it is the impact of coming up against religious doctrines and Judaism-specific cultural ligatures at home [5], contending with the consequences of both external and internalized homophobia and transphobia [6–8], or navigating the ways in which queerness and Judaism conflict both inter- and intrapersonally [9, 10], our personal narratives and innermost emotional and psychological landscapes are inevitably subject to these elements.

In order to gain an in-depth understanding of the intimate worlds of queer Jews, it is vital to hone in on these more private experiences and the lessons (both enlightening and disruptive) that they teach. After all, as discussed in the previous chapter, there will always be myriad ways of comprehending and negotiating even the most predictable and consistent environments (e.g. conservative Jewish spaces). My interviewees' understandings of themselves and their place in the world are not only influenced by that world but are also dependent on their individual perspectives and both intergenerational and personal histories. This chapter will explore these factors and the ways these narratives affect peoples' inner worlds.

Families, Faith, and Histories

Dahni: Growing up [I remember] learning about my grandparents' experiences [in the *Shoah*], but also getting older, [I recognize] how their survival manifested in how they lived their lives and how that's affected my mother. And how it affected her brother. And [now I'm] understanding [that] part of that has actually also affected me.

Before we explore more internal and individual experiences, it is important to consider the role of families. Families often form a bridge between one's individual life and the greater culture(s) or society you exist within [11, 12]; they are a collective interpretative lens which can have significant impact on how you might view yourself and the world around you. This is particularly true when considering Jewish families living in diaspora, whose historical narratives are often interwoven with traditions, traversals, and tragedies which set them apart from the society they live within. It would be negligent to discuss Jewish families without directly addressing the role of the *Shoah* (Holocaust), particularly considering that many of my interviewees were descendants of survivors. Though I've described families as bridges between individuals and the society they live within, the *Shoah* has transformed this bridge from something which facilitates free bilateral passage into something more closely resembling a drawbridge over a deep moat. The spectre of the *Shoah* haunts even those families whose members have been spared any direct connection to those historical atrocities; it acts as a ward against complacency and relaxation, and a kind of fear-based force which drives many Jewish families to prioritize self-protection and insularity [13, 14].

I distinctly remember discussing my grandmother, who is also my namesake, with my mother. She and I share many things, including our love for food and the large bodies this food was used to maintain. But there is something in Shoshana's relationship with food that was unmistakably informed by her experience escaping a concentration camp at the age of 12. An early conversation about this with my mother highlighted that Shoshana's relationship with food was not one of jest and celebration, something beyond the old saying "they tried to kill us, we won, let's eat" [15]. It was more akin to "they tried to kill us, and they will again, eat every meal as if it's your last". Although Shoshana passed away when I was just a toddler, this is absolutely something that was passed down to me, whether through epigenetics or the subtle ripples this attitude caused down generational lines within my family.

I'll be discussing food and its role in Jewish life in more details in the next chapter; however, this anecdote provides us with a significant piece of insight into a core aspect of the Jewish family psyche: we can never rest or leave ourselves unprotected, and we must remain vigilant of any violence that may come against us again. It is undeniable that this fear is the reason we have guards at synagogues, and undoubtedly it is also the driving force for the actions of the Israeli government, all of which are done in the name of "Jewish survival". It is impossible to ignore such a visceral guiding principle, particularly considering the outcomes of its distortion through the lens of conservativism and fundamentalism. Having discussed the implications of this persecution narrative on a broader global scale in the previous chapter, I will now explicate on the impact that this rigid narrative has within the smaller and more intimate arena of the (Jewish) family.

Many of my interviewees discussed coming up against their family's traditions and faith. Rigidity around preservation of Jewish culture manifested in familial pressure and conflict, which affected how my interviewees navigated their life. For many, breaking away from the strict boundaries of Jewishness required effort,

Madelaine: The Israeli government is horrendous, and they're committing crimes. They're acting in ways that Jews have been treated, and they're [en]acting that upon Palestinians.

Shosh: What does your [. . .] connection to Judaism look like for you?
Ariel: Some days it feels like. . . it looks like obligation.
[. . .]
Shosh: What do you mean when you say that?
Ariel: I felt, particularly in my teens and my 20s, quite an obligation to uphold certain values and even choices. Deciding to eat pork and getting tattooed were really big choices for me to kind of step out of that obligation and do things that I wanted to do.
Natan: In more alternative or queer communities [. . .] we don't have to be talking about [. . .] or questioning these things like gender or sexuality or other political things. In a way, it's not political, it just is. It's not a question. It's just accepted. [. . .] [Whereas] when I'm, for example, at family dinner, it becomes a philosophical political discussion, which is annoying. I don't really want it to be that, I just want it to be normal.

even bravery, and was often done with the knowledge that fallout from these choices could very well result in a loss of place within that family. This breaking away could be as simple as abandoning practices of Kashrut[1] or, as was the case for several of my interviewees, beginning to explore and come into their queerness. Even for people I spoke with who maintained good relationships with their families, the spectre of religious and cultural tradition continued to loom, particularly with regard to gender and sexuality. While most did not experience out-and-out rejection, they nonetheless came up against the cis-heteronormativity which has become entrenched within mainstream Jewish culture [16, 17], and the kind of questioning around queerness which often positions queer and trans people as somehow less deserving of a place in the home (family or otherwise) [18].

Although this kind of conflict is not something which is exclusive to Jewish families, it does carry a particular set of issues with it, especially when the notion of survival is introduced into the mix. Jewish survival has become synonymous with (particularly Israeli) nationalism [19], the preservation of the "old life world" of pre-World War II Jewish communities [20], and biological reproduction [21], all of which run counter in one way or another to the lives and perspectives of many queer and trans peoples. I am not trying to uphold the notion of the queer as the *Stranger*, the *Perpetual Radical*, or the *Eunuch*; many queer people subscribe to nationalist ideals, are fully immersed in some of the most queerness-supressing and oppressive cultures and belief systems, and both belong to and continue biological lineages and families. Nonetheless, if queer cultures and documented narratives have taught us anything, it is that our nations, conservative belief systems, and biological families are highly prone to shunning us and seeking to reduce or eliminate any traces of our sexualities and non-conforming gender experiences[2] [22–24].

Honing in on conflict within the family, it is important to consider that for most queers it isn't even a matter of one's personal experiences and perspectives of gender or sexuality being at odds with those of one's parents or siblings or other family members. The mere label of "queer" or "trans" carries with it a certain level of scrutiny and othering which wholly discounts

---

1   The rules dictating which foods, artefacts, and rituals are aligned with Jewish laws.
2   If you are queer and find yourself baulking at this statement, feeling it is untrue of your own country, faith, or family, I invite you to consider the ways in which you may be positioned within those systems: is your race or citizenship status favoured in your country? Are your faith and cultural traditions ones which generally uphold, or at least avoid villainizing, queerness? Do you have a supportive biological family or other queer biological kin?

or overlooks the minutiae of one's inner world, or at a minimum causes a kind of disruption which family members must then overcome, often experienced as a kind of grief process [25]. These labels become a blockade to relationality, particularly within families which are aligned with homophobic or transphobic values, either explicitly or implicitly. In a way, queer people *stop making sense* to their relatives and have to earn their way back into their families through a kind of self-explaining process of *re-legibility*. This is a kind of *queer labour* which underlies many family (and non-family) relationships, even those which could be viewed as supportive and understanding.

> *Ariel:* With my loved ones, with my friends, with my family, it's really difficult to see them struggle and misgender me, and then having to sometimes, particularly initially, do a lot of work about looking after them in that.
>
> *Shosh:* So [. . .] you're having to play support even though you're in an unsupported sort of position.
>
> *Ariel:* Yeah.

Queerness continues to be understood as a familial cul-de-sac, despite the reality of many queer and trans people having biological children of their own [26], including some of my interviewees. This view of queerness is a particularly jagged point of contention within Jewish families; a queer family member signifies the end of a lineage, a kind of failure to carry on the vital work of Jewish reproduction [27]. In a way, this feeds into the notion of "completing Hitler's work

> *Justin:* Around the time of finishing school everyone was in this very selfish kind of mode of "what am I gonna do with my life?" So then to throw [coming out] on top of it was a big deal.
>
> *Shosh:* Did it feel disruptive?
>
> *Justin:* Yeah, yeah definitely. It felt exposing.

for him" [28] which is so often touted in discussions of having children within interfaith marriages, particularly those where the mother is not Jewish, thereby severing the matrilineal line which is supposed to carry Jewishness through to the next generation. This positions queer Jews as more than just a confusing figure in a normative family; it puts us up against the very tenets of Jewish survival discussed in an earlier paragraph. If you cannot or will not have children, or if your children will not be matrilineally Jewish (e.g. due to the lineage of your surrogate or IVF donor), you are risking being viewed as going against Judaism itself. Between the Torah specifically dictating the mitzvah of פְּרוּ וּרְבוּ (*be plentiful and multiply*) and the post-Shoah fears around dwindling numbers of Jews, it is easy to see how queerness becomes a betrayal to the Jewish family. It extends beyond the usual family conflict that heterosexuals may encounter if they choose not to reproduce [29], and becomes a political, spiritual, and cultural issue.

Beyond the issue of biological reproduction, the otherness of queerness can also pose a threat to the reproduction of Jewish culture writ large. There is an inherent unknownness in queer culture, a big and vibrant question mark over many of the facets of life that traditional Judaism has already written an answer in for. We don't know if poppers are Kosher, we certainly mix our meat and our milk[3], and most of our collective social time happens outside the home on Shabbat. Queer culture forms a porthole to people and groups with myriad lived experiences which may bring into question some of the fundamental pillars of Jewish life, and could lead us astray! These concerns of course carry within them the same homophobic, transphobic, racist, anti-substance use positions which permeate Australian culture more broadly, but with the added twist of the *survival of the Jewish people* seemingly hanging in the balance. This makes exposing oneself as queer or trans to one's Jewish family all the more complex and concerning. It also often makes it harder to even simply witness one's own queerness or transness within a Jewish context. With that in mind, it is important to discuss the experience of coming in and coming out.

Coming In and Coming Out

In my previous writing, I've used the term *coming in* as a counterpoint to *coming out* [30]. This phrase carries with it some important distinctions in my personal perspective on the experience of queerness and transness, as well as amplifying the aspects of sexual and gender self-discovery that are often lost when we remain focused on coming out. Coming out is about others; it is a plea to the world to understand us, an act of coming forward that remains trapped somewhere between a confession, a leap of faith, and an act of defiance. Coming in is about ourselves; viewing our inner world as a house with many rooms, one in which we spend a lifetime exploring. When we neglect to consider how we *come in* to our sexuality and gender(s), we relegate our most interior comprehensions of ourselves as things which need to be negotiated with our family, friends, and societies we live in.

There is also a kind of essentialism that tends to creep in when others become obsessed with a person's "need" to come out. I distinctly remember a moment in 2012: I was at an interstate punk festival where my bands were performing, and found myself in a conversation with an ex-lover who had come out since our mutually closeted affair some months prior. He proceeded to

---

3 Take that as you wish.

tell me, "You *have* to come out, just do it! Tell people you're gay!" I felt a dis-comfort that, at the time, I attributed to my own shame about being gay, as well as living in a relatively small city with a very meagre and intimate (and highly heterosexual) music scene. The obsession with my coming out became something I internalized, and not long after I found myself disclosing what I perceived to be my sexuality at the time to most of the people in my life. But this was nowhere near the end of the road, and in many ways my very public announcement of who I thought I was at the time signalled the start of a years-long process to fully reconfigure my understanding of my sexuality and gender.

I often joke that I've inhabited nearly every letter in the LGBT+ alpha-bet soup, but this joke is slightly soured by the fact that each "letter" came with a painful period of *re-coming out*. I felt obligated to inform others of who I was and who I wanted to fuck at each stage, afraid that a lack of disclosure would position me as disingenuous, secretive, or two-faced. At the same time, I allowed little space for myself to explore those sexual and gender positional-ities, as my focus was on ensuring that I was upfront with others at all times. I would argue that most of the time, people had assumed or had more insight about my gender and sexuality than I did, with many of my multiple "coming outs" being met with some variation on the theme of "duh".

Yes, there was a sense of defiance in my perpetual honesty, but it was less about personal satisfaction and much more about what I felt was socially and politically correct to do. After all, I'm old enough to remember celebrities being outed by activists in the 90s and early 00s [31], and the subtext these actions carried with them: being in any way visible or publicly known and not being upfront about your queerness is *bad for the queers*. Even though I was just a little pisher from Nowhereseville, I'd been touring regularly since I was 20 and felt the pressure to put queerness on the map in my own small way, in my tiny punk corner of the world. But I'd spent so long shouting my queerness from the rooftops that I forgot to breathe.

Whenever I did come up for air, which would be every few months or years, I'd find myself *coming in* in ways that would surprise me: my faggyness turned into trans lesbian-ism; my sissyness became femme womanhood which then became butchness; my relationship to masculinity and femininity and their sexual relationality continues to evolve as I age and

Elite: I identify as a lesbian now by virtue of the fact that if any-body sees me they would con-sider me a lesbian. G-d forbid if anything should happen to [my wife]. . . Whether I'd be with a man or woman, I actually couldn't tell you 100 percent.

learn about myself. Any notion of a singular gendered or sexual decree which

could be easily read out to the masses via coming out has been truly ameliorated by my internal experiences of coming in. Even in reading this, you may
find yourself developing an idea of what my "final form" is. You might be viewing this paragraph as a kind of coming out, an explication of a trajectory with a
conclusive start and endpoint. But I assure you that is not the case; the person
writing these words is not who you will find should we ever meet.

Jonathan: I had a very clear sense that I did not want to be a teenager in high school and deal with high school dating. I did not want to be a teenage girl being seen as a potential date by teenage boys. I also knew that I was not going to grow up to be a woman who dated men. I knew clearly that I was never going to be anyone's girlfriend and I knew that I was never going to be anyone's wife. [. . .] So I just thought okay if I tell everyone I'm a lesbian, that will take it off the table and I can just sidestep all of that high school drama stuff.

Many of my interviewees had also gone through this kind of metamorphosis. Their route to queerness and transness was not a straight line but a series of questions, conflicts, and relational dynamics which formed zig-zags, spirals, oscillations, and other shapes which are impossible to verbally describe. To shave down our understanding of these experiences to a "coming out story" would be doing them a great disservice, yet at the same time coming out continued to play a significant role in the lived experiences of my interviewees. These are two truths that must be held simultane-ously in our minds: *coming out* is not the only important process in developing a relationship with one's queerness; and at the same time, *coming in* is inextricably linked with experiences of disclosure, exposure, and navigation of other people's perceptions and feelings regarding your queerness.

Early Experiences and Turning Points

Perhaps it is most useful to view *coming in* and *coming out* as two quotients which make up the greater whole of queer growth. Certainly, many of my inter-viewees' earliest instances of connecting with their queerness were a blend of the two factors. Moments of early queer intimacy or self-discovery were often interwoven with the spectre of societal prejudice, if not directly disrupted by a person holding those prejudiced views. To be queer is to be vulnerable, to push through fears which many hold but few confront. I do not consider it fatalistic or stereotyping to discuss fear with regard to queer and trans lives, particularly in the context of early experiences of exploration. Fear is a reality for most queer people, though its prominence in our life narratives expands and contracts. To grow up in the kinds of families, communities, and societies we have discussed so far is to grow up with an understanding, however shadowy, that those things within us which eventuate in queerness carry significant consequences. It's therefore imperative to name fear and to consider how our lives are shaped by it, while also taking into account the ways queers have harnessed its power to our advantage [32].

Although I argue that fear forms a significant aspect of early queer experiences, I would also argue that its effects and our interpretation of those effects are much more primordial to begin with. I could not name something as concrete as "I feel fear about this aspect of myself" until well into adolescence, but there was an affective atmosphere of confusion and unease which underlined most of my young life. Several of my interviewees expressed experiencing this kind of wash, a blanket encasing many early experiences which could only be described as "difference" or "otherness". Sometimes it feels like fumbling in the dark, like trying to make out the shapes of shadows. Other times it feels like sleep paralysis, like being out of control and having forces exerted on you that your dream-state self cannot fully comprehend. Being a queer kid often means being a confused kid, a young person who can sense the alienation of queerness without the capacity to make it make sense.

Ariel: When I came out, unfortunately, that wasn't my choice. I had a best friend in early high school who was a cis queer young woman. We [. . .] had a bit of crossover between friendship love and romantic love. It was really easy for us to have sleepovers. Her mom walked in and called my mom in regards to us [. . .] fooling around. And so I kind of got busted at quite a young age.

These abstract sensations eventually metastasize into what we can call fear: others' fear of us, our fear of others, and our subsequent fear of ourselves. They form a self-oscillating loop, amplifying each other to form screeching howls only quelled by intervention, by quietening, and by introducing some kind of stabilizing force back into this closed system [33]. These quietening elements are often accidental, ephemeral; a conversation with an older queer, an item of clothing bearing the gift of gender euphoria, or a book or internet thread that seems to reflect your experiences word-for-word. These elements are cumulatively healing, rather than individually curative, meaning that we often spend our early

Hunter: My sister told me this story that when I was in Grade 3, they asked us to [. . .] just make up a story, and I wrote in a male character. Apparently, I have no idea, quite unusual for a kid at that age. So this kind of stuff was coming up quite early. There was no conversation in [. . .] 1992 about gender in kindergarten and stuff. So I didn't have the language. I didn't understand. I didn't know why anyone was bullying me. I didn't know . . . I didn't understand why my experience was so different.

(and later) lives searching for them, amassing enough fleeting queer curios to form a shield against this overwhelming estrangement from the world. When an amplified guitar goes into feedback, the only solution is for someone or something to turn down the volume [34]. The same applies here. We cannot stop the cycle of fear all by our lonesome, and certainly we are met with many life experiences which only make the noise of homophobia and transphobia louder and more shrill. In order to dampen the noise, to interrupt the self-feeding cycle of fear, we need a disruption.

When talking with people about their experiences of queer self-discovery and self-realization, I often get a sense that in many people's minds there exists a kind of multiverse, a series of what-ifs or untraveled roads which would have created a vastly different reality to the one the person is currently in. These *hidden realities* [35] can seem incredibly concrete; we can almost feel ourselves embodying those alternate selves, the versions of us who took the other turn at the fork in the road or stuck to the path we were assigned without ever looking for an exit. At times I find myself almost witnessing an alternate self, or a younger self who has yet to glean what I have since learned of myself. I see those alternative trajectories as clear as day: the other me who stayed with an abusive partner who had gone out of her way to suppress my queerness; the other me who never came across a copy of Stone Butch Blues; the other me who never understood the reason for trying to kill their current self over and over again.

The affects of these insights into the lives I could have lived are what I would define as the devastation of a life lived unqueerly. That is not to say that a life lived queerly is not rampant with devastation. After all, we all regularly encounter people and systems who are hellbent on destroying us specifically for our queerness. Rather, it is about the particular

Jamaica: [it took a while] to feel settled enough to even come forward and say for sure that I was bisexual. Because prior to that I was like, "maybe one day I'll just end up with a guy and it'll be fine. No one will have to know". And then like later I [thought] "oh, my G-d, what a sad little like life scenario I set out for myself where if I'd just been okay dating guys that no one would ever have to know, I could settle down and have a child, it would be great". It's not exactly what I want for my life.

Shosh: So did it feel kind of disingenuous in some way?

Jamaica: Yeah, absolutely. [I] tried to fit the mold of [. . .] what I thought a heterosexual couple would be like. I had this sort of idealized view where it was all just like: boyfriend, girlfriend, falls in love, gets engaged, meets family, has kids. [I thought] maybe that's what I want. I tried to act that out and G-d, I was so unhappy from those first couple of moments and I didn't understand why. And I kept telling my friends, "I'm too gay for this shit". Like, I can't relate to any of this, this is not what I want.

devastation that comes from an absence of a relationship with oneself, with one's truths and complexities and capacity to exist beyond the ligatures of an oppressive world. Observing these alternate realities feels like a close call, like narrowly avoiding a head injury when falling in the shower. It is a kind of near-death experience, in that the misery of that smaller and emptier life feels like it's mere inches away, a looming threat we avoided by the skin of our teeth. The desolate or stark feelings attached to these contemplations of an unfulfilled queer life are not unlike the "No-Thing-ness" that we merge with in death [36], except that unlike real death we see our alternate selves trapped in the doorway, between living potential and the complete darkness of our actual demise.

The spectre of a life lived in twilight produces a broad range of affects: relief at our escape, fear of perhaps one day having to return there, and motivation to save others from that fate. Even for those of us whose coming in/out experiences were rather mundane or relatively free from fear, there is a sense of negotiating

Justin:
[my coming out] was generally unsurprising [to others] but that doesn't mean that it wasn't traumatic and difficult at the same time.

queerness as inevitably traumatic. It is that distinct and irreversible shift that Catherine Malabou [37] discusses; the trauma is built into the fact that the person's inner and outer world is permanently altered, having formed new synapses and relational dynamics that cannot be undone. In a sense, our contemplation of our non-queer alternate universe selves is a recognition of the compromising exchange made in the process of coming in/out. We trade the safety of anonymity for the challenge of self-knowledge, the comforting simplicity of superficiality for the dark and bottomless depths of complexity, the stability and predictability of linear narratives for the often rocky path less travelled. Coming in/out is not simply a matter of self-liberation or a pursuit of authenticity; rather, it is stepping into an alternate dimension where curiosities and what-ifs are materialized, with all their incalculable consequences.

Madelaine: I realized the way [my queerness] impacted people around me meant that I had to take some ownership of that feeling. So in a lot of ways I would identify as butch but that's more a shortcut. I get mistaken for a man a lot. It's uncomfortable and awkward. I'm okay with myself but I need to find people around me [who are the same] because it can be destabilizing, so how do I restabilize myself in it? I surround myself with other people who identify as masculine of centre and who understand this experience and find community in it.

How then do we anchor ourselves in these queered alternate dimensions? How do we make sense of a world that seems so similar to the one we just left, yet is coloured so vividly by the transformative impact of coming into our queer selves? My interviewees experiences were laden with these scattered ciphers, random and ephemeral encounters that signposted their arrival in this new reality. Yes, water was still wet and the ground still stood below the sky, but so many other things were suddenly different. This dimensional shift can feel maddening; why is it that only I have noticed these radical metamorphoses? Everyone around me seems unaware that the scene has changed so dramatically. Parents, friends, colleagues, teachers – all are going about their business in this new world as if nothing has happened.

I may be showing my age, but I find these feelings to be most comparable to the experiences of the dimensional travellers depicted in shows such as the mid-90s interdimensional travel sci-fi show Sliders [38]; all the players are the same, but their narratives have been significantly rewritten. Celebrities become pariahs, loving parents become strangers, and so-called societal truths are ameliorated or subverted. Perhaps most importantly, you have no way of returning to your previous dimension, to the way things were. As the opening monologue to season 5 says:

> "What if you found a portal to a parallel universe? What if you could Slide into a thousand different worlds? Where it's the same year, and you're the same person, but everything else is different. And what if you can't find your way home?" [39]

Maddy: Since coming out as queer I kind of re narrativized my life and said "oh I was always gay". And then I was just trying to deny it or like had been the victim of compulsory heterosexuality. But I think it's not bad to say that I was straight at this time and then I was bisexual at this time. And then I was queer and lesbian attracted to women and non-binary people at another time.

How do our intrepid interdimensional explorers familiarize themselves with their newfound reality? Through connecting with those in the know, people who are aware of the structures of this new dimension, and sometimes even other people who have themselves gone through a wormhole or two. These connections are not always amicable, sometimes even outright dangerous, but they nonetheless gesture towards the underlying context that one has arrived at. For many queer people, the shift might not be as startling as arriving on a version of Earth where dinosaurs still roam the planet [40] or aliens have invaded [41], but the difference between our pre- and post-queered world is nonetheless stark.

Having come into our queerness, we suddenly find ourselves in a world laden with context and subtext where seemingly there was none before. Undoubtedly, there is a sense of fear, or at the very least trepidation; the cycle of fear discussed earlier in the chapter becomes illuminated, as we come to understand just how heavily our sexualities and genders are politicized and marginalized in the broader world. But there is another element at play, one which encapsulates the disruption required to break the yoke of the cycle of fear that this world so desperately wants us to bear. This element is pleasure, in all its many facets: joy, curiosity, wonder, and exhilaration. Like the many faces of G-d expressed through *hayyot ha-qodesh*[4] [42], or Angels, so too do we encounter queer pleasure in many forms across our life. As I've discussed in previous writing [43], (queer and trans) pleasure runs directly counter to the traps of fear, shame, and misery laid out by this world. Sometimes pleasure presents itself as something so small that we can miss it if we do not pay attention to it; other times, it's as blatant as a billboard. A long-awaited first kiss, a beautiful dress, an act of protection from homo/transphobic harm by another, a meaningful tattoo [44] – all these are opportunities for pleasure to enact its antidotal power over the venom of queer shame.

In entering this new-but-not-so-new reality of queer self-discovery, there are many perils, but like our interdimensional travellers will attest, there are also many allied powers. There are people who are sympathetic to your experiences, places where your way of life has been maintained despite the odds, sources of knowledge which can enlighten you on the ways of navigating this "new" world. In fact, it is these processes of inquisitive exploration, of trying to come to grips with your altered surroundings, that are often the most life-saving aspects one has access to in their early stages of gender and sexuality exploration.

> *Margie:* So when I was a kid, if somebody would have said to me, "you can be attracted to men, women, or both", I probably would have been a lesbian [earlier]. Do you know what I mean? And also, [. . .] I'm cis-gender, but if somebody would have said [a similar thing] about gender diversity, [who knows?] You can't know your options unless you know them.

I do not necessarily believe that a queer "community" is what assists us, particularly when considering the many ways so-called communities continue to exclude their most marginalized members [45–47]. Instead, it is a sense of *communion*, of relating to the world in ways which seek connection, mutuality, self-exploration, and a deepening understanding of the

---

4 This roughly translates to "Holy Beasts".

Hunter: I identify as a trans man and I identify as straight, in that those are the words that kind of make the most sense. [...] I think words tend to kind of ... I can't remember which philosopher it was that said this but [...] the words flow over the top of experience, they skirt over the top. [...] It's not a fixed connection.

injustices enacted in this reality. For me, this meant that I *did* leave that homophobic partner, I *did* come across a copy of Stone Butch Blues, and I *finally* figured out that so much of my suicidal misery was borne of frustration with my body and how both I and others related to it. These turning points came about through conversations with confidantes, through books and zines and records and online forums, and through my hodgepodge of spiritual practices manifesting unexpected insights. These are all acts of communion, of attenuating oneself to what is being offered, and to seeing the potential in traversing routes shrouded in mysterious fog rather than remaining on the highway of normalcy.

Queer New World

Jonathan: [After transitioning, I started] feeling like I was actually a part of society and could contribute to society. I started to do more in the way of volunteering and [...] taking on roles that I wouldn't have thought that I could do in the past. [...] Prior to transitioning or taking steps in that direction I really just was an intellectual entity.

Having discussed the early experiences of queerness, with their myriad facets and affects, I believe it is essential to conclude this chapter with a consideration of the experiences of those who have spent some time immersed in their queerness. It would be a misrepresentation of queer and trans lives to suggest that the river of experience is made up entirely of rapids and waterfalls, constantly foaming and entirely resistant to any kind of settlement or serenity. Indeed, we may spend much time in upheaval; several of my interviewees had complex experiences around negotiating family dynamics, social circles, and other life aspects that are inevitably touched by one's growing relationship with one's queer sexuality or gender. But there was tranquillity too; many people I spoke to had found anchor points, either internal or external, which buffered them against the tumultuous world around them. For some it was having children, or a long-term partner, or even simply becoming settled in their self-understanding. For others there was a sense of calm amidst what many may perceive as constant unsettlement; their sense of self was contingent on the understanding that they exist in flux, and this understanding in itself brought peace.

Too often, discussions around queerness and transness produce discourse which either oversimplifies any sense of queer permanence (e.g. the notion of being "born this way" [48]) or positions early experiences of sexual or gender exploration as something finite with definitive end points (e.g. perceptions of gender transition as a simple matter of medical and aesthetic shifts as opposed to a radical transformation [25]). There seems to be a constant drive to bracket queer and trans lives into digestible narratives with a beginning, middle, and end. In truth, these are attempts at capturing an uncatchable beast, of trapping a ghost[5]. Queerness is simultaneously easier to sit within and more in flux than current broad societal narratives can ever understand. This is partly because, at its core, queerness is a kind of daily, moment-to-moment practice; it touches every aspect of one's life, if one allows it. It is much like the effects that certain spiritual practices can have, where even a moment of engagement can colour a person's entire week [49].

Sally: Once I started exploring myself and going trying to find a more authentic self it didn't stop and just [became what] I've called the "topsoil effect". I dug through the first layer and there's another layer and another layer and another layer underneath. And I had to keep digging and well, [I'm] still digging. It seems like it gets closer to bedrock and then something else turns up. But maybe that's part of the excitement of life.

In that sense, queerness can become a kind of *permanent practice of impermanence*. We are constantly mindful of the ways the world interacts with people like us, particularly those of us who cannot or will not conceal or downplay our queerness or transness. We are often attuned to the spectre of transphobia and homophobia, to the highly permeable boundaries between our inner personhood and the world's reactions to it. Conversely, we are also aware of the mismatch between the richness of our inner worlds and the reductionism that has become so dominant in a supposedly increasingly queer-friendly world. The concept of "LGBT communities" in and of itself plays a role in this reduction, a conceit which conflates vastly different life experiences based on a single axis of difference, that of existing outside of cisheteronormativity [50, 51]. We are therefore constantly buffeted, not so much by our queerness but by its relationship to the world(s) we inhabit as queer people. Being immersed in one's queerness therefore means forming a relationship with these shifting undercurrents, becoming familiar with the geography of the streams we traverse, and transforming ourselves into expert sailors[6] as we bob and weave with the waves.

---

5 Without the necessary Ghostbusting equipment.
6 Or pirates, depending on your preference.

There are of course other factors which play into how well we navigate these sometimes treacherous waters. Class, race, disability, and the sheer lottery of whatever nation-state one finds themselves born into or living in all affect the "smoothness" of our sail. While I did not specifically seek out this information when talking with my interviewees, it was nonetheless clear that all these factors affected their practices of navigating the world. Some interviewees had supportive families but were significantly affected by racial or class-based issues, while others had little-to-no support but benefitted in some ways from how they were understood by others in the world (e.g. being seen as cis or white) or by other factors in their background, such as their access to wealth. This too is why queerness sits at this nexus of permanence and impermanence; it is not a separate entity, but one organ within a wider system, constantly affecting and being affected by those other factors. Even if that organ is settled, other disruptions to the system will be felt throughout the body, and the same is true for when queerness is what is causing discomfort in an otherwise unperturbed organism.

To perceive queerness in this position is to gain a better understanding of why investigating queer lived experiences is such a fickle process. I would argue that taking a viewpoint on queerness that simply states that it contains multitudes is in itself an understatement; queerness is more akin to a Calabi-Yau manifold [52], a form that expresses itself differently from different angles, revealing more dimensions than we can digest from a singular perspective. The same was true for my interviewees, whose queerness and transness morphed in their nature when it was attuned to at different places or points in time. Sometimes it was a small object that needed to be kept in one's pocket; other times it was a blinding light engulfing the entire space it occupied. As I will explore in the proceeding chapters, this same multi-dimensional experience applies to Jewishness too (chapter 5), and perhaps becomes more prominent at points where queerness and Jewishness meet (chapter 6). As you read through these chapters, this perspective on multidimensionality – as opposed to volatility or unpredictability – will become increasingly vital in understanding the intersections of these lived experiences.

References

[1] Wachtel PL. *Cyclical Psychodynamics and the Contextual Self: The Inner World, the Intimate World, and the World of Culture and Society.* London: Routledge, 2014. Epub ahead of print 21 April 2014. DOI: 10.4324/9781315794037.

[2] Sandhu D, Tung S. Identity formation in relation to family environment. *Read Appl Psychol* 2006; 245.

[3] Cote JE, Levine CG. *Identity, Formation, Agency, and Culture: A Social Psychological Synthesis*. Psychology Press, 2014.

[4] Lapsley D, Hardy SA. Identity formation and moral development in emerging adulthood. *Flourishing Emerg Adulthood Posit Dev Third Decade Life* 2017; 1: 14–39.

[5] Pomson A, Schnoor RF. *Jewish Family: Identity and Self-formation at Home*. Indiana University Press, 2018.

[6] McNeil J. An Exploration of Transgender People's Mental Health.

[7] Cornish MJ. The impact of internalised homophobia and coping strategies on psychological distress following the experience of sexual prejudice.

[8] Ong C, Tan RKJ, Le D, et al. Association between sexual orientation acceptance and suicidal ideation, substance use, and internalised homophobia amongst the Pink Carpet Y Cohort Study of young gay, bisexual, and queer men in Singapore. BMC *Public Health* 2021; 21: 1–11.

[9] Etengoff C, Daiute C. Family members' uses of religion in post–coming-out conflicts with their gay relative. *Psychol Relig Spiritual* 2014; 6: 33.

[10] Shilo G, Yossef I, Savaya R. Religious coping strategies and mental health among religious Jewish gay and bisexual men. *Arch Sex Behav* 2016; 45: 1551–1561.

[11] Bermudez JM, Mancini JA. Familias Fuertes: Family resilience among Latinos. In: Becvar DS (ed). *Handbook of Family Resilience*. New York, NY: Springer, pp. 215–227.

[12] Beitin BK, Aprahamian M. Family values and traditions. In: Nassar-McMillan SC, Ajrouch KJ, Hakim-Larson J (eds). *Biopsychosocial Perspectives on Arab Americans: Culture, Development, and Health*. Boston, MA: Springer US, pp. 67–88.

[13] Bar-On D, בר-און ד. *Fear and Hope: Three Generations of the Holocaust*. Harvard University Press, 1995.

[14] Silverstein J. "If our grandchildren are Jewish" heteronormativity, holocaust postmemory and the reproduction of Melbourne Jewish families. *Hist Aust* 2013; 10: 167–186.

[15] Koltun-Fromm K. Imagining the Jewish God.

[16] Silverman RE. Coming out, becoming, being, and doing: A spectrum of LGBT and female Jewish identity in contemporary culture and a call to action for the Jewish community.

[17] Anders C. Transformed Before God. *Tikkun* 2005; 20: 59–62.

[18] Fortier A-M. Making home: Queer migrations and motions of attachment. In: *Uprootings/Regroundings Questions of Home and Migration*. Routledge, 2003.

[19] Zerubavel Y. The "Mythological Sabra" and Jewish past: Trauma, memory, and contested identities. *Isr Stud* 2002; 7: 115–144.

[20] Inowlocki L. Grandmothers, mothers, and daughters: Intergenerational transmission in displaced families in three Jewish communities. In: *Between Generations*. Routledge, 2005.

[21] Keysar A, Kosmin BA, Scheckner J. *Next Generation, The: Jewish Children and Adolescents*. SUNY Press, 2012.

[22] Slootmaeckers K. Nationalism as competing masculinities: Homophobia as a technology of othering for hetero-and homonationalism. *Theory Soc* 2019; 48: 239–265.

[23] McDermott E, Gabb J, Eastham R, et al. Family trouble: Heteronormativity, emotion work and queer youth mental health. *Health (N Y)* 2021; 25: 177–195.

[24] Wilets JD. Religion and homophobia. *Wiley Blackwell Encycl Gend Sex Stud* 2016; 1: 1–5.

[25] Riggs DW, Rosenberg S, Fraser H, et al. *Queer Entanglements: Intersections of Gender, Sexuality, and Animal Companionship [in press]*. Cambridge: Cambridge University Press, <https://www.cambridge.org/core/books/queer-entanglements/7B3392D8A210207E4D221 0A1A9E76715> (2021, accessed 16 February 2021).

[26] Mamo L, Alston-Stepnitz E. Queer intimacies and structural inequalities: New directions in stratified reproduction. *J Fam Issues* 2015; 36: 519–540.

[27] Caron D. My Father and I: Jewishness, queerness, and the Marais. *GLQ J Lesbian Gay Stud* 2005; 11: 265–282.

[28] Mehta SK. *Beyond Chrismukkah: The Christian-Jewish Interfaith Family in the United States.* UNC Press Books, 2018.

[29] Marshall H. *Not Having Children.* Oxford University Press, 1993.

[30] Rosenberg S. Coming in: Queer narratives of sexual self-discovery. *J Homosex* 2018; 65: 1788–1816.

[31] Chekola M. Outing, truth-telling, and the shame of the closet. *J Homosex* 1994; 27: 67–90.

[32] Harris A, Holman Jones S. Feeling fear, feeling queer: The peril and potential of queer terror. *Qual Inq* 2017; 23: 561–568.

[33] Jenkins A. Self-oscillation. *Phys Rep* 2013; 525: 167–222.

[34] French RM. *Engineering the Guitar: Theory and Practice.* Springer Science & Business Media, 2008.

[35] Greene B. *The Hidden Reality: Parallel Universes and the Deep Laws of the Cosmos.* Penguin UK, 2011.

[36] Bailey LW, Yates J (eds). The no-thing-ness of near-death experiences. In: *The Near-Death Experience.* Routledge, 1996.

[37] Malabou C. *The Ontology of the Accident: An Essay on Destructive Plasticity.* Wiley, 2012.

[38] Pilot. *Sliders.*

[39] The Unstuck Man. *Sliders.*

[40] Dinoslide. *Sliders.*

[41] Invasion. *Sliders.*

[42] Schafer P. *Hidden and Manifest God, The: Some Major Themes in Early Jewish Mysticism.* SUNY Press, 2012.

[43] Rosenberg S. Why Pleasure? In: Riggs DW, Ussher J, Robinson K (eds). *Transgender Reproductive and Sexual Health: Presents and Futures.* Routledge, In Print.

[44] Rosenberg S, Sharp M. Documenting queer(ed) punk histories: Instagram, archives and ephemerality. *Queer Stud Media Pop Cult* 2018; 3: 159–174.

[45] Riggs D. Queer theory and its future in psychology: Exploring issues of race privilege. *Soc Personal Psychol Compass* 2007; 1: 39–52.

[46] Athelstan A. Queer feminine affect aliens: The situated politics of righteous femme anger at racism and ableism. *Feral Fem* 2015; 3: 90–105.

[47] Wang-Jones T "Tie" S, Hauson AO, Ferdman BM, et al. Comparing implicit and explicit attitudes of gay, straight, and non-monosexual groups toward transmen and transwomen. *Int J Transgenderism* 2018; 19: 95–106.

[48] Behrensen M. Born that way? The metaphysics of queer liberation. *APA Newsl Philos Lesbian Gay Bisexual Transgender Issues*; 12.

[49] Hanh TN. *The Miracle of Mindfulness, Gift Edition: An Introduction to the Practice of Meditation.* Beacon Press, 2016.

[50] Mizock L, Hopwood R. Conflation and interdependence in the intersection of gender and sexuality among transgender individuals. *Psychol Sex Orientat Gend Divers* 2016; 3: 93–103.

[51] di Bartolo AN. *Is There a Difference? The Impact of Campus Climate on Sexual Minority and Gender Minority Students' Levels of Outness.* ProQuest LLC, 2013.

[52] He Y-H. Calabi-Yau Spaces in the String Landscape. *ArXiv200616623 Hep-Th*, <http://arxiv.org/abs/2006.16623> (2020, accessed 9 March 2022).

· 4 ·

REINVENTING TRADITION: HOLY DAYS, ARTEFACTS, AND NOSHING

If engaging with both Jews and non-Jews about Judaism over the years has taught me anything, it's that there are as many entry points into these discussions as there are seeds in a pomegranate. Jewishness as an ancient culture, as pop culture, as cuisine, as an aesthetic, as a religion – all valid and fascinating aspects which can produce hours of discussion and exploration. I found the same to be true when talking with my interviewees about their experiences as Jews, especially when exploring the parts of their Jewish experience which shone brightest or weighed heaviest. I have done my best to form a kind of pyramid[1] in arranging this chapter, beginning with aspects of Jewishness that are more personal and internal and moving up through the layers as the chapter progresses.

Food

For many of my interviewees, food played a significant and multifaceted role in their Jewish life. Food was a comfort, a point of connection, an inheritance, a conscious process that required their full attention and dedication. Sometimes

---

1 Pardon the Pesach pun.

Dahni: I used to do [a Seder] with my cousins and one year they couldn't do it for some reason and I was like "but we can't not have Seder". So I did it myself. Never doing it again coz it's a stupid amount of work.

Shosh: It's a lot of work!

Dahni: Well I hadn't thought about things so I actually minced the fish myself to make the gefilte fish. And then found out afterwards from the older people in my life, "No you just buy it, you get them to mince the fish in the fish shop". But nobody told me that!

Liv: My grandmother on my dad's side [. . .] converted. [. . .] So she learned all these recipes from her mother-in-law, and my mom learned them from her mother-in-law. And it's kind of like a really nice thing. [. . .] The culture is not just like "you have to pray and you have to not eat pork, and you have to do this". It's like no, part of the culture is actually within the food as well, and that's something that like I like I love because it's just so special.

the importance rested with the fact that the food was specifically Jewish food; other times, it was simply the process of cooking, eating, or sharing a meal with others that provided this type of physical and spiritual satisfaction. Understanding a person's relationship to food often forms a gateway to other understandings. What is their family like? How did they grow up? What else nourishes them? It's impossible to disentangle these experiences from the cooking that fuels and reinvigorates these life aspects.

Food forms an ancestral bond, a powerful connection point to collective Jewish memory that extends from our ancient past to our present-day lives [1]. Jewish food is about stories – from fables to morality tales to historical narratives which have left an indelible mark on the lived experience of all Jews. It's no wonder that one of the defining text of Jewish law is called Shulchan Aruch [2], which translates to "a set table". Since so much of Jewish history has revolved around food (or its absence), eating has become a kind of microcosm for Jewish life more broadly. Within food we see expressions of relational ethics [3], spiritual practice [4], and the evolution of Jewish traditions and culture [5]. The motivations, practices, places, and timings of Jewish food consumption have been documented for millennia [6], and reflect everything from climate variation to class differences to what has or has not been canonized in our ever-expanding body of knowledge. If there is indeed a collective Jewish Body (as discussed in an earlier chapter), then its intake will inevitably become a matter of great importance.

In the previous chapter I mentioned my personal intergenerational inheritance regarding food: my grandmother Shoshana, a Shoah survivor, approached every meal as if it was her last. Food was not only central to her life but also a sustaining force. Every story I have of my grandmother involves her cooking mounds of food, feeding her family and guests until they cannot eat anymore, and being ever-ready to prepare more should someone still be hungry. Sometimes she would force my mother and her siblings to finish their meal, often in cruel ways. An unfinished meal was worse than a sin; it was a kind of betrayal. For Shoshana, eating was not about spirituality, or even nourishment to a certain extent, but about survival. Having escaped a concentration camp at 12, I have no doubt that my grandmother developed a relationship with food that most of us cannot

Madelaine: I don't keep kosher but I think [food] represents a form of connection and hospitality hat I think is important. And I don't necessarily enact that myself. I'm not a great cook, I don't have massive dinner parties. But I Feel the importance of going to a Passover meal and I feel the connection that comes when you're together around food

fathom; food deprivation in the camps and its psychological impacts have been well documented [7, 8]. Talking about food was a survival mechanism, exchanging recipes even when one had no way of preparing and eating those dishes became a life-preserving feat that touched all those who lived under the dehumanization, enslavement, and threat of extermination by the Nazi regime [9]. Food talk remains a means of spiritual survival and act of resistance for many marginalized and displaced peoples today, most notably for Palestinians who have been dispossessed by the Israeli government [10]. Even in the absence of access to traditional and culturally satisfying food, the mere mention of it is enough to enliven spirits and reconnect with ancestral knowledge.

Food, specifically sharing food, is one of the strongest connective tissues of Jewishness, both to other Jews and to the broader world. Our cooking is our way of creating an interactive space that is focused on mutual pleasure. When we nosh[2] together, we are truly together. Within these experiences, our food carries knowledge that is passed down through generations [11], and with it a set of lessons about our relationship to the lands we live on, the cultures we are surrounded by (or at times the cultures which have conquered our people), and the ethics that are detailed in our holy books. The dispersion of Jews across

Sally: When I was maybe about 10 or something, [my sister and I] were getting a bit hungry on Yom Kippur, and of course you're not really supposed to eat anything, but Mom said fair enough and drove round ... Couldn't seem to find any sandwich shops or anything, there weren't a lot of Maccas or whatever in those days. And what did she end up buying us? Ham sandwiches for lunch. So no we're definitely not orthodox.

Shosh: I was waiting for that punchline!

2 Yiddish word for eating.

the world, a result of endless pogroms and mass exiles, meant that we had to find ingredients where we could, come to terms with our relationship to those ingredients (e.g. are they Kosher), and inevitably subsume those ingredients into the ever-expanding category of what one might define as "Jewish food". This includes "Australian" Jewish food; there is a rising tide of Jewish cooks and chefs sharing their recipes and specific experiences as Jews in Australia, such as that of the Monday Morning Cooking Club [12]. The plethora of Jewish food is so vast that it requires a literal encyclopaedia [1] just to get even a glimpse at the innovation Jewish peoples have had to develop as they landed in whatever region they were currently welcomed or at least accepted in. Jewish food is also an archive of "vanished worlds", with dishes and ingredients that speak to cultures and communities which no longer exist [13].

In response to this continual displacement, many food-based practices have become in one way or another focused on inviting in others, and particularly inviting non-Jews into our ceremonial spaces. Our teachings indicate that we should feed strangers, whether Jewish or otherwise, especially if they are marginalized or in dire straits [14, 15]. This is not to say that Jewish law regarding food and Kashrut has not been, at times, specifically utilized as a way of distinguishing the supposed superiority of Jewish practices to those of gentiles [16]. But as Jewish food continued to evolve into a range of culinary styles, rather than strictly a set of rules regarding preparation and consumption, non-Jews inevitably became more included in Jewish cuisine and food practices [17]. The liminality of Jewish food, a cuisine that is nearly always informed by adjacent cultures, also suggests a kind of permeability between Jewish and non-Jewish peoples; Jewish cooking often influences and is influenced by the communities and cultures Jews find themselves immersed in, and this synthesis creates a vibrant point of inter- and intra-cultural connection [18].

Although there are multiple positive aspects of Jewish connections to food, our relationship with food has gone through a kind of corruption, especially as a result of the Holocaust, as was the case with my grandmother. Yes, having access to food is something to be proud of and to rejoice in, but our relationship to food can at times become flattened into something that is more historical and symbolic than ever-present and embodied. In other words, rather than experiencing food, we often *think* about food. I see this in the ways my own experiences of disordered eating often distorted my concept of food, turning it from a source of enjoyment to something I needed to ration out, or make the most out of. Whether I was portion-controlling or getting second helpings and licking the plate to the point of being sick, food became less about sustenance and pleasure and more about a set of compulsions centred around what was "good" or "bad" about eating[3]. The ways in which food-related trauma leaks through generations is an undercurrent of Jewish life that has become codified into our culture through humour and acts of remembrance, but its legitimate impact on our lives often goes unspoken [19].

We eat bitter foods as a reminder of our suffering on Pesach, we fast on days of mourning, but while these may be read as an embedding of negativity into our eating nothing could be further from the truth. These customs still encourage embodiment and reflexivity, and view food as sustenance that must be engaged with consciously. Simmering below these, however, is a truer indication of the distorted relationship many of us have formed with food over the past century in particular. It's what Susan Bordo's sister Binnie Klein wrote of in their shared essay "Missing Kitchens" [20]; the post-World War II erosion of our willingness to fully relish in food in our daily living, and the decreasing role that eating plays in our lives outside of its pure functionality. Our kitchens, once the centre of any Jewish family home, have become blurred and often neglected spaces, along with the meals prepared in them. There are many factors at play here, beyond the impact of the Shoah; Feminist pushback against the compulsory cooking foisted on women for centuries by Jewish law [21] and Capitalism writ large [22][4], as well as the ever-slimming amount of spare time that many people are able to dedicate to home cooking as opposed to other alternatives[5] [24], especially people who experience socioeconomic issues or other structural barriers to "healthy" food access [25, 26]. That is to say, the "missing kitchen" is not strictly a Jewish phenomenon but rather the Jewish experience of that phenomenon holds particular political and historical narratives within it.

Slam: If I'm at pre-drinks for the club [. . .] I often will bring food. like I've done soup a lot lately because it's winter. And I'm like "eat before you go out". My Jewish friend that I mentioned earlier commented and said it was a very Jewish thing. And this is where it may tie into transness in Judaism is the maternal Jewish role like stereotypically of the grandmother or the mother. You know with the food and making the home warm and shit like that. I really resonate with that connection and [. . .] that role.

---

3 For example, whether leaving food on the plate was wasteful, if I was eating too many calories, what foods were "healthy" or "unhealthy".
4 Which in many cases has not been supplemented through men taking up the mantle of family cooking [23].
5 Such as takeaway food or pre-made meals.

Shosh: I've had a few people now talk about food. And it felt like even for people who were, for various reasons, relatively distant from community or even distant from really over identifying as Jewish themselves, food was still really sort of primary. Do you feel like it's like a connective thing?

Ariel: It's huge. And it reminds me ... Sometimes if I'm having a really good day and I feel really joyous I wanna eat food that I grew up eating, and then other days when I'm feeling a bit sad, I might be homesick. I might be missing my mother, my sister, I'll go out and eat that food.

Despite this, many of my interviewees seemed thrilled to discuss food with me, particularly in the context of their Jewishness. It almost feels like we are entering a kind of Renaissance, a reclamation of the place food plays in our lives. Its interconnectivity with memory, comfort, identity, and community was a highly evident thread running throughout many of my interviews. The majority of my interviews took place in cafes, dining rooms, and restaurants, and even if food was not consumed while we spoke, its presence was often felt through aromas, nearby cutlery, menus, and so on. It is evident that no matter how much disruptive force is exerted on Jews' relationship with food, we return to it time and time again.

Shabbat

Shosh: Have you experienced any milestones that have brought you deeper into Judaism in any capacity.

Maddy: I think definitely [...] starting Shabbat, not regularly but the times we have done it, and also the Pesach last year with the queer Haggadah, that was definitely [a point where I] felt like a Jew.

While food as a general theme was quite prominent, it was especially present in its connection with celebrating Shabbat. There is a kind of movement at play here, from the more embodied acts of cooking and eating to the more overtly spiritual and communal experiences which encompassed Jewish life for many of my interviewees. Shabbat dinner in particular forms a nexus of Jewish experiences: for some, it is a holy time of initiating our connection to the divine spirit of Shabbat and its decree of rest and recovery; for others, it is a designated time of week set aside for sharing time and space with our loved ones, regardless of its degree of overt religiousness; for most, it's some combination of the two. Whether the process is followed to a tee, with all required blessings, or is simply a Friday night meal, Shabbat is a galvanizing action between Jews and their family (chosen or otherwise) [27].

Shabbat means different things to different people and is highly contextual in terms of how it is experienced. I have personally conducted Shabbat in a wide variety of ways: alone in a hotel room in Norway, with a tealight and two bread rolls I bought from a supermarket; with several Jewish friends, replete with a lavish home-cooked feast followed by an equally lavish feast of various illicit substances; as the sole Jew, translating each line of prayer from Hebrew to English in order to include the non-Jewish attendees; as well as many other iterations. At its core, these were all conscious and intentional acts of celebrating Shabbat, but the underlying emotions and sensations differed widely. Respectively, I felt internally connected to a bigger force all by my lonesome in Norway, at ease and in deep communion with my Jewish friends, and like an ambassador of Jewishness in those contexts where I was the only Jew and the only person with a direct spiritual connection to the actions being undertaken. Even if I wanted Shabbat to be the same every week, it is impossible. My environment, company, and inner state all feed into how this millennia-old ritual plays out.

Jamaica: We do Shabbes every now and then. But it felt more like family dinner. We light the candles, we say [the prayers], but it would be kind of just a part of the process. Because we also have family dinners on Fridays with just my mom and my dad and I. and that would have no Shabbes [rituals], nothing. But it still [has] the same feel to me.

Holy Days

The same kind of heavy contextualization that affects how Shabbat is conducted seems to permeate throughout all Jewish celebrations. If we are going to discuss the notion of "missing kitchens", we may as well consider the *missing Menorah, missing Seder plate*, or the *missing Sukkah*. That is to say, our relationship to our traditions and their related material artefacts and spaces have undergone a process of quietening, of being sidelined, or of being outright denied to us either by internal or external forces [28]. While some of my interviewees grew up with all traditions fully intact, it was still evident that certain depths and dimensions of these experiences were often missing. Holy days were either arbitrary or irrelevant, or at least seemed to be discussed that way in my interviews. In contrast, other interviewees grew up with minimal Jewish Holy Day celebrations, if any at all, and their

Justin: I'm one of three [siblings]. I've got two sisters, I'm the middle. So one older one younger. We all went to Jewish day school. Not really, not a particularly religious one but still very sort of I think culturally affiliated. So we do all the high holidays, all the festivals [. . .]. That's roughly it in a nutshell. So [. . .] we're secular but traditional, I think is the way I'd broadly describe us.

connections to those celebrations often seemed to be experienced through this lens of disruption.

In some ways, it seems that this fracturing of our relationship to traditions, whether through the inevitable processes of diaspora or the denouncing of Holy Days as an extension of a family's divorce from religiosity, is in itself a part of the Jewish experience. Our relationship to our Jewishness is ever-evolving, with Holy Days presenting a particularly fertile ground for discovering where we sit with our ancestry, our present, and arguably our future [29]. Discussions of Jewish traditions often encircle around notions of inheritance, of furthering a culture and/or faith, and of having a sense of duty to our families. However, our relationship to Holy Days and other traditions form a litmus test of all these aspects, with our actions gesturing to much more than these superficial ideas about the correct way to survive and preserve our peoples through specific customs. In other words, those things that we may feel are Jewish about ourselves cannot be measured through simple metrics such as strict adherence to this or that tradition. In fact, it is the ways we resist, challenge, or redefine these traditions that is often the most Jewish thing we can possibly do.

Coming In to Jewishness

In the previous chapter I explored the notion of *coming in* to our queerness and transness. Coming in is an active process, a lifelong journey of attenuating ourselves to ourselves through various internal and external processes. However, it is not a process that is limited to gender or sexuality; I would argue that every aspect of one's identity that causes intra- or inter-relational rupture, difference, friction, or complexity is something that necessitates unpacking and (re)configuring within ourselves. As I've written previously, there is a fine balance between transformation and conservation that seems baked into Jewishness [30]. Questioning our position in relation to Jewishness is par the course for the Jewish experience, despite it being considered a risky process – one which certain scholars suggest could lead us away from Judaism if pursued without the necessary awareness and caution [31]. Yet here we are, millennia down the track from the formation of our peoples, and we still consider questioning, in its myriad forms, to be a vital aspect of Jewish existence. We ask questions in our rituals, we interrogate the meanings of the Torah, we are often drawn to practices and occupations which encircle a pursuit of new knowledge. At times this pursuit may lead us away from what we might consider faith, as it did for thinkers such as Spinoza. But even in those instances, Jewishness remained a part of the pursuit of questioning; it was simply reframed from a matter of faith to one of culture, ethnicity, or a mode of inquiry [32]. In overtly introducing queerness and transness into Jewish theology, we are merely expanding preexisting processes of imagining and reimagining [33].

Jewishness may be something that we enter into[6], either by birth or by conversion, but there is more to the journey once we have passed through the gate. It is an experience of movement, at times of discomfort, and often an embodied experience of the inevitable flux that exists in a culture that is several thousand years old. Context is often key, and plays out quite dramatically in Jewish existence. Our bodies, personalities, life histories, families, friendships, and the societal structures we exist within all affect the flow of the river through which we travel Jewishly. Throughout this stream are bottlenecks, dams, and floodplains; spaces where we can fully immerse ourselves in the waters of our Jewishness and others where the current slows down to a piddle. That is to say, our relationship to Judaism is never constant, always shifting and changing depending on our personal circumstances. But whether the water overwhelms us like a gushing rapid or is simply a puddle we splash across on our way elsewhere – the substance remains the same.

Not to strain this metaphor, but I would argue that at times traversing the currents of Jewishness feels less like sailing or swimming and more like a Herzogian effort – pulling a vessel over waterless terrain just to continue on our journey [34]. Several of my interviewees mentioned experiencing periods of complete detachment from their Jewishness, whether as a result of their personal beliefs or conflicts between themselves and others in their Jewish community. If Jewishness is a stream of water, then these experiences left my interviewees navigating arid terrains with not a drop in sight. And yet it seems that even those who found themselves travelling this barren landscape eventually discovered an oasis; a body of water that appeared to be ostensibly

Jamaica: I got the weirdest flak from my friends at Jewish school and synagogue because I wasn't choosing to do my Bat Mitzvah. I was basically ostracized to the point where I decided to not go anymore because, you know, I would come home and mom would be like, "why are you upset?" I'm like, "no one talked to me, mom", and she would be like, "why aren't your friends talking to you?" And I'm like, "I have no clue". And then later on in my years, I [. . .] realized that [. . .] I just didn't belong with them anymore. Like they were sort of pushing me away because I had chosen to not do that.

---

6 Or arguably, something which enters into us.

detached from any running stream which nonetheless provided opportunities for immersion.

My connection to Jewishness from my teens and well into my 20s felt not unlike that of Herzog's accursed actors (may their memory be a blessing); having any connection to Jewishness felt like a hard slog, a Sisyphean task of pushing ship/shit uphill, at times to such an extent that I abandoned my efforts completely. My mother's position of being "an Israeli, not a Jew" certainly contributed to this detachment; we did not celebrate any Holy Days, Shabbat was rarely if ever mentioned, and all discussions of Jewish faith happened in an intellectual context rather than one of practice and spiritual potentiality. I understand her position, and in many ways I believe I have covered in a previous chapter why so many people, including my mother, arrive at that mindset. Israeli nationalism, post-Holocaust survival instincts, political opposition to religious fundamentalism, as well as my family's specific connection to Bhagwan Rajneesh aka Osho have all played a part in our distancing from anything that would be perceived as a religious practice. Shoshana 1.0, my mother's mother, strictly divorced herself from Judaism specifically and G-d in general, no doubt as a result of her horrific experiences in concentration camps [35]. This separation too is an inheritance that cannot be under-emphasized in exploring contemporary Jewish experiences.

But my drive to connect with Jewishness still trickled away beneath the surface. In fact, it was my experience of coming in/out as queer that finally drove me to explore these undercurrents of faith that still existed within me. I'd spent years reading books on Buddhism, Hinduism, Satanism, Discordianism, Wicca, and other non-Jewish paths to spirituality. I was always obsessed with spirituality and yet felt unable to find the proper vessel to contain these deep desires. Much of the queer content I was consuming, particularly in my early days as an out queer person, was also at odds with my experience of faith. Queer punk bands and zines (justifiably) rejected G-d and organized religion wholesale, and though they often targeted Christianity specifically [36], nonetheless there was little room for discussions of faith in the context of queerness.

Sally: I suppose I'm a very diverse intersectional person. Adding in all the bits of me. And there is some connection to those more natural elements. Maybe there's a very autonomous part of me that likes this sort of Wiccan Pagan approach which doesn't have so much structure. Whereas of course Orthodox Judaism, I mean not that I was ever Orthodox, is incredibly structured in where men and women have to sit, and what they can and can't do etc. Whereas there isn't that sort of structured, control freak type of approach in belief systems like Wiccan pagan[ism].

All of this was changed by a little zine I came across years before called TimTum [37]. The zine is a punk-tinged exploration of transness and queerness as they related to Jewish tradition and faith. It is beautifully illustrated with monstrous queers and transsexuals who were everything I ever wanted to be. I'd actually found the zine in my late teens, and would regularly read it, but after coming out at 24 and rediscovering it in my bookshelves the publication took on a whole new meaning. Suddenly I could see the sinew between all of these seemingly disparate forces bubbling up inside me: my gender, my sexuality, my connection with G-d, all playfully interacting across the pages of this tiny zine. It was not long after that I'd decided to attempt to return to synagogue, though this would prove to be a much more complex process. Nonetheless, the dam had broken; I could no longer deny my relationship to my Jewishness, in the same way I could no longer deny these other aspects of myself that I'd spent so long suppressing.

I will explore the interconnections of Jewishness and queerness further in the next chapter, but this example nonetheless elucidates a fundamental element of the process of coming in which both these identities share: the unpredictable nature of those forces beyond ourselves that can jostle those things inside us that we've kept on a dusty shelf or relegated to an attic or basement. The zine was not the only thing I chanced upon that motivated me to *come into* my Jewishness: an invitation by a stranger to attend a service while shopping at a Jewish deli; the Jewish musicians I discovered as my music taste expanded and deepened; a conversation about Jiu Jitsu with a Rabbi; an unpleasant "altercation" with a group of Neo Nazis at a punk show[7]; all these experiences (and more) hinted at a core aspect of myself that held power, complexity, and uniquity which I needed to attend to. Having trudged through a spiritual desert, I was pushed by unexpected forces towards an oasis. Feelings of loss were replaced by a sense of connection and belonging; in the same way, the parched throat and cracked heels of those lost in the desert are soon quenched and moisturized at the shore of a water haven.

I am writing this in the lead-up to Pesach, and so the tale of travelling the desert en route to a holy Jewish place feels particularly poignant, maybe even a little bit cheesy. But it's true; there is a kind of Jewish persistence present across my interviews, and within my own life, a connection to Jewishness that seems to behove us to push forward and find our way into a personal relationship with this culture and faith. There is something deep inside us that drives

---

7 Don't worry, I won.

us to discover, recover, and often reinvent our Jewishness. In fact, in order to understand how coming in manifests itself Jewishly, it is the latter sense that is particularly worth focusing on.

Discovering, Recovering, Reinventing Jewishness

Elsa: I think Pesach is also really political, which I really love. And not only is it political, but it has the ability to evolve in in a way that I think is really special. Maybe I don't have that many points of reference for other cultures or religions in the ways that they integrate, you know, contemporary issues into their holidays or celebrations. But I think it's beautiful that Pesach allows a space for us to discuss contemporary human rights issues and even the use of the Seder plate and how that's evolving to incorporate, you know, issues around queerness and Palestine. [...] It feels like it's such a family cultural bonding experience, but also inherently political, in a way that I find really meaningful for me.

Although Judaism has always been iterative in nature to one degree or another, the past century has certainly highlighted this aspect in new and sometimes revolutionary ways. The proliferation of alternatives to the traditional tracts of Judaism, such as the Sha'ar Zahav LGBTQ-friendly Siddur [38] or the Israeli Black Panthers Haggadah [39], touch upon a malleability and responsiveness that forms an undeniable aspect of Judaism. All rules of Judaism, every piece of Talmudic writing, have been structured in response to the conditions of their time. The Shabbat prayer has alternative phrasing for when one does not have access to wine [40]; we construct ephemeral boundaries to allow freedom of movement on Holy Days and Shabbat [41]; people who are sick or at risk of illness are exempt from potentially harmful customs such as fasting on Yom Kippur [42]. Every tradition holds fail-safes within it that rely on individual and group contexts. It is therefore unsurprising that for many of my interviewees, their engagement with the traditions of Judaism reflected all the nuances of their personal lives and histories.

For some of my interviewees, moulding Jewish traditions was an overtly political act. Whether the rituals and traditions were modified to be more inclusive of other marginalized peoples, or to further embolden my interviewees' as people who are themselves marginalized, the process of actively reshaping or recontextualizing these centuries-old words and actions seemed to produce deeper meanings and provided more power than simply reciting things as they have been dictated all this time. There is a genuine sense of reclamation here, particularly for those of us who have been neglected by or rejected from more traditional communities.

Reformulating, re-evaluating, and rectifying aspects of Jewish tradition that do not align with our lived experiences provide a bridge between two opposing polarities: total abandonment of Jewishness as a means of honouring the other aspects of one's identity, and total suppression of those seemingly incongruent aspects in service of maintaining a normative sense of Jewishness. This dichotomy appeared time and time again throughout my interviews, with a broad range of lived experiences that pitched a person's Jewishness against other parts of their personhood. But as I discussed earlier in the chapter, questioning runs deep within the Jewish experience, and that includes the questioning of this rigid dichotomy. Additionally, as with the processes of *coming in* that I have been exploring throughout this book, we do not simply stop at questioning. Exploring and challenging preconceptions surrounding any aspect of our personhood inevitably leads to action.

The actions we take to oppose or challenge the inflexibility of normative Judaism is not simply a matter of finding loopholes in texts [43], though this may provide an inroad towards more radical changes, particularly for those of us who have been raised more religiously. Rather, it is a matter of considering

Jonathan: I studied theology at university and one of the things that I studied was the Hebrew wisdom literature. [. . .] My lecturer [. . .] specialized [. . .] in feminist analysis of the Hebrew Bible and was particularly interested in the way that the wisdom literature was kind of looking at the domestic sphere and the way that wisdom was characterized as a woman; and that wisdom was the feminine knowledge [. . .] of the natural order and the domestic order that was [. . .] the counterbalance to knowledge of law and Torah. And that was [. . .] how I got interested in getting more religious. [. . .] My Hebrew name comes from Proverbs 31, the Eshet Chayil. And that's a piece of the wisdom literature that I really connect with. Speaking about the qualities of women [. . .] as strong and having good business acumen. We as a same gender couple, me and my partner, two men together, it's a tradition that we have adopted to both sing that together. [. . .] It's a song that's traditionally sung by a man to his wife on Friday night. And we sing it together to each other because we think that it sums up all of the qualities that anyone would want in a partner.

which words and acts serve us and which require rewriting, recomprehension, or removal. Resources such as Trans Torah [44] and the Queer Mikveh[8] Project [45] are significant examples of reworking Jewish traditions as a means of validating and supporting contemporary experiences of Judaism which are not

8 The Jewish ritual of self-purification through water immersion.

addressed in traditional texts. Elsewhere, there are Rabbis and other members of Jewish communities who are challenging even the holiest of Jewish places, namely the synagogue. Thinkers and spiritual leaders such as Rachel B. Gross and Miriam Terlinchamp have worked to reconceptualize arguably the most central pillar in traditional Judaism by refuting the importance of brick-and-mortar temples, forming and reconceptualizing spaces of Jewish culture and faith which are more ephemeral and responsive to the lives of contemporary Jews [46, 47].

Natan: You can define [Jewishness] in ways that suit you. And I think that's pretty well accepted as well. Like you can be all types of Jews, and there is this, I think for the most part, acceptance of the spectrum, and other ways you can reason with that, which is just really fun. It's really experimental.

The work of these people and groups, alongside countless others, might be seen as a distortion or dilution of Judaism, cherry-picking what is convenient and eschewing what might be difficult. But this could not be further from the truth. Tradition often provides comfort, making its disavowal or abandonment a potential source of unease, if not outright hardship. Take, for example, the complexity of experiencing loss: Jewish tradition can offer great comfort to the ones in grief through the processes and perspectives our faith has held over centuries regarding the passing of loved ones [48]. Questioning these deeply entrenched beliefs about death and mourning would hardly constitute a matter of convenience, either on a personal or social level. Moving outside the boundaries of tradition often means being caught in liminality, wrestling with our thoughts, and feeling without the respite of familiarity, structure, or the kinship that they often generate. I often describe this uncomfortable liminality as feeling like doggy-paddling in the middle of a pool while others rest on the concrete. What else keeps us afloat but effort?

Hunter: In terms of how I live my daily life, it's much more about what is going on in my brain rather than what I'm doing in the external world. [. . .] It's like, [Jewishness] is a thing that's drip-fed to you. Culture is drip-fed to you and it structures your life in a way that you cannot appreciate until you're with people who don't live their life that way.

It is clear then that these actions I have been discussing are not oriented towards simplicity and superficiality but rather are processes of inquisitiveness that seek the complexity and depth underlying Jewish lived experiences. When we move away from viewing Judaism as a set of rules and towards understanding it as a lens through which we see the world [49], these acts of modification and reimagining begin to make a lot more sense. Jewish culture, Jewish humour, Jewish beauty, Jewish faith – these are all revealed through contrast, comparison, and contemplation, not simply through capitulation to pre-established rules. It is almost cliché to invoke the notion that you ask two Jews and get three opinions [50], but it bears repeating when we consider some of the more radical shifts that are taking place within many Jewish households and communities. The Jewish lens centre around acknowledging our internal conflicts, our paradoxical views, and the friction between the elements which make up who we are as people, families, and communities.

Most importantly, there's a reason why you ask two Jews and get three opinions, rather than ask one Jew and get two opinions. We form our worldviews relationally, through interacting with others who at the very least share this core value of questioning. I would even go as far as to argue that despite the concerns expressed by Drob [31], who I cited earlier, amongst others, our connection to Jewishness is formed and often strengthened relationally even when the people or text we relate to are not Jewish. Who is the person haranguing these two poor Jews for their three opinions for the last few centuries? One can argue that a person is a catalyst for their inevitable debate, making their request for commentary a vital part of the resulting set of conclusions. The asker is undefined, except by their act of questioning; they may not be a Jew, and yet their presence produces Jewish discourse.

Dahni: Because [Jewishness is] important my partner tries to bring out aspects of it. So she's decided that we have a tradition now of lighting the candles every night for Hanukkah which I did growing up but haven't done as an adult. And I actually really like doing it but I would never think of doing it myself. So the fact that she's kind of gone "well now we should do this, isn't it on right now?". And she also refers to me as a bad Jew because I never remember these things. And she's totally right, I normally find out from other people.

I have certainly found this to be true in my personal life. Many of my most Jewish moments were instigated by, supported by, or shared with non-Jews. My experiences were not less Jewish by virtue of their involvement of non-Jews or elements that exceeded the limits of Jewish scriptures. Undergoing my first Mikveh in the presence of my non-Jewish partner at the time did not diminish the spiritual connection I experienced at that moment. Eating a cheeseburger for Shabbat does not take away from my immersion in the spirit of rest and restitution. My friend bringing a cake to an otherwise unleavened Pesach event did not take away from the communal experience we all shared during that Seder. The proof that these are not supposedly "tainted" or "impure" lies in my inner experience: in those moments I have experienced joy, affinity, pleasure, and Holiness. They did not feel less-than because they sidelined Halakha or included participants who did not share my ancestral connection to the traditions being engaged with. They created exactly what I wanted them to create – a space for me to be as I am, and to immerse myself in spirituality exactly as I wished to.

References

[1] Marks G. *Encyclopedia of Jewish Food*. HMH, 2010.

[2] Lauterbach JZ. The Origin of the Shulchan-Aruch.

[3] Gold N. Let all who are hungry come and eat: Food ethics, tzedakah, and how we celebrate. In: Zamore ML (ed). *The Sacred Table: Creating a Jewish Food Ethic*. CCAR Press, 2011.

[4] Abusch-Magder R. Food preparation as a holy act: Hafrashat challah. In: Zamore ML (ed). *The Sacred Table: Creating a Jewish Food Ethic*. CCAR Press, 2011.

[5] Sussman LJ. The myth of the Treifah Banquet: American culinary culture and the radicalization of food policy in American Reform Judaism. In: Zamore ML (ed). *The Sacred Table: Creating a Jewish Food Ethic*. CCAR Press, 2011.

[6] Cooper J. *Eat and Be Satisfied: A Social History of Jewish Food*. Jason Aronson, 1993.

[7] Bachar E, Canetti L, Berry EM. Lack of long-lasting consequences of starvation on eating pathology in Jewish Holocaust survivors of Nazi concentration camps. *J Abnorm Psychol* 2005; 114: 165.

[8] Rappoport L. *How We Eat: Appetite, Culture, and the Psychology of Food*. ECW Press, 2010.

[9] Slaw TP. *On Holocaust Cookbooks: Fourth Generation Jews and the Re-creation of Jewish Food Culture*. Thesis, University of Kansas, <https://kus chol arwo rks.ku.edu/han dle/1808/27937> (2018, accessed 16 March 2022).

[10] Meneley A. Eating Wild: Hosting the Food Heritage of Palestine. *PoLAR Polit Leg Anthropol Rev* 2021; 44: 207–222.

[11] Gavin P. *Hazana: Jewish Vegetarian Cooking*. Hardie Grant Publishing, 2017.

[12] Chalmers MF. *Monday Morning Cooking Club: The Food, The Stories, The Sisterhood*. Hardie Grant, 2011.

[13] Horowitz E. Remembering the fish and making a tsimmes: Jewish food, Jewish identity, and Jewish memory. *Jew Q Rev* 2014; 104: 57–79.

[14] Tzoref S. Knowing the heart of the stranger: Empathy, remembrance, and narrative in Jewish reception of Exodus 22:21, Deuteronomy 10:19, and Parallels. *Interpretation* 2018; 72: 119–131.

[15] Goldstein (Rabbi.) W. *Defending the Human Spirit: Jewish Law's Vision for a Moral Society*. Feldheim Publishers, 2006.

[16] Rosen-Zvi I, Ophir A. Goy: Toward a genealogy. *Dine Isr* 2011; 28: 69–122.

[17] Waterman S. *Eating, Drinking and Maintenance of Community: Jewish Dietary Laws and Their Effects on Separateness.* Springer Netherlands, 2014, pp. 2867–2880.

[18] Kravya V. *Tell Me What You Eat and I Will Tell You If You Are Jewish: Food and Discourses of Identity Among Thessalonikian Jews.* Doctoral, Goldsmiths, University of London, <https://research.gold.ac.uk/id/eprint/28537/> (2003, accessed 22 March 2022).

[19] Chesler BE. Implications of the Holocaust for eating and weight problems among survivors' offspring: an exploratory study. *Eur Eat Disord Rev* 2005; 13: 38–47.

[20] Bordo S, Klein B, Silverman MK. Missing Kitchens. In: *Twilight Zones: The Hidden Life of Cultural Images from Plato to O.J.* University of California Press, 1999.

[21] Gardner SM. The Good Woman Makes the Empty Kitchen Full: The Culinary and Cultural Power of Women in the Sephardic Jewish Diaspora.

[22] Seccombe W. The housewife and her labour under capitalism. *New Left Rev* 1974; 3–24.

[23] Neuhaus J. *Manly Meals and Mom's Home Cooking: Cookbooks and Gender in Modern America.* JHU Press, 2012.

[24] Mills S, White M, Brown H, et al. Health and social determinants and outcomes of home cooking: A systematic review of observational studies. *Appetite* 2017; 111: 116–134.

[25] Janssen HG, Davies IG, Richardson LD, et al. Determinants of takeaway and fast food consumption: A narrative review. *Nutr Res Rev* 2018; 31: 16–34.

[26] van Kesteren R, Evans A. Cooking without thinking: How understanding cooking as a practice can shed new light on inequalities in healthy eating. *Appetite* 2020; 147: 104503.

[27] Marks LD, Hatch TG, Dollahite DC. Sacred practices and family processes in a Jewish context: Shabbat as the weekly family ritual par excellence. *Fam Process* 2018; 57: 448–461.

[28] Altman AN, Inman AG, Fine SG, et al. Exploration of Jewish ethnic identity. *J Couns Dev* 2010; 88: 163–173.

[29] Greenberg I. *The Jewish Way: Living the Holidays.* Jason Aronson, Incorporated, 1998.

[30] Rosenberg S. "Lehadlik": Radical Jewish music, gender and disidentification in Aviva Endean's work. *Dir New Music*; 1. Epub ahead of print 24 May 2018. DOI: 10.14221/dnm. i2/2.

[31] Drob SL. Judaism as a Form of life. *Tradit J Orthodox Jew Thought* 1988; 23: 78–89.

[32] Smith SB. *Spinoza, Liberalism, and the Question of Jewish Identity.* Yale University Press, 1997.

[33] Ladin J. In the image of God, God created them: Toward trans theology. *J Fem Stud Relig* 2018; 34: 53–58.

[34] Fitzcarraldo. *Adventure, Drama, Werner Herzog Filmproduktion, Pro-ject Filmproduktion, Filmverlag der Autoren,* 1982.

[35] Bîderman Š. *Wrestling with God: Jewish Theological Responses during and after the Holocaust.* OUP USA, 2007.

[36] Limp Wrist. This Ain't No Cross on My Hand. <https://genius.com/Limp-wrist-this-ain t-no-cross-on-my-hand-lyrics> (2004, accessed 4 April 2022).

[37] Bazant M. TimTum – A Trans Jew Zine.

[38] Congregation Sha'ar Zahav. *Siddur Shaar Zahav: The All-Inclusive Siddur*. Congregation Sha'ar Zahav, 2009.

[39] The Black Panthers. *The Israeli Black Panthers Haggadah*. Jewish Currents Press, 2022.

[40] Weinstein YS. Grape juice: The solution to prohibition. *Tradit J Orthodox Jew Thought* 2015; 48: 19–32.

[41] Rapoport M. Creating place, creating community: The intangible boundaries of the Jewish "Eruv". *Environ Plan Soc Space* 2011; 29: 891–904.

[42] Taub I. The Rabbi who ate on Yom Kippur: Israel Salanter and the Cholera Epidemic of 1848. *You Shall Surely Heal Albert Einstein Coll Med Synag Compend Torah Med* 2009; 295.

[43] Stein E. *Rabbinic Legal Loopholes: Formalism, Equity and Subjectivity*. Columbia University, 2014.

[44] Trans Torah. Trans Torah. *Trans Torah*, <http://transtorah.org> (2018).

[45] Cunningham ZL, Erev R. Simple Queer Mikveh Guide.

[46] Judaism Unbound. Judaism Unbound Episode 113: Embrace the Weird – Miriam Terlinchamp. *Judaism Unbound*, <https://www.judaismunbound.com/podcast/2018/4/4/judaism-unbound-episode-113-embrace-the-weird-miriam-terlinchamp> (2018, accessed 5 April 2022).

[47] Judaism Unbound. Rachel B. Gross: Judaism unbound episode 278 – The Deli is my synagogue. *Judaism Unbound*, <https://www.judaismunbound.com/podcast/episode-278-rachel-gross> (2021, accessed 5 April 2022).

[48] Silverman E. Finding comfort in grief through Jewish tradition. *Illn Crisis Loss* 1991; 1: 20–26.

[49] Klein M. Teaching about Jewishness in the Heartland. *Shofar* 2014; 32: 89–104.

[50] Laytner AH. *Arguing with God: A Jewish Tradition*. Jason Aronson, Incorporated, 1977.

· 5 ·

ELSEWHERENESS, LANDLESSNESS, AND QUEER JEWISH SOLIDARITY

As you will have noticed by now, I find it almost impossible to discuss Jewishness without considering its queerness and queerness without considering its Jewishness. While both aspects vary widely in how we experience and understand them, they nonetheless dovetail in undeniable ways historically, relationally, and internally. This chapter will provide an exploration of these experiences of "hyphenated selves" [1] and the ways these elements come together to form a singular but complex lifeworld. From the onset of this project, I wrestled with how it is best to frame my underlying aim, alternating between describing it as an exploration of "experiencing Jewishness queerly" and that of "experiencing queerness Jewishly". As this chapter will show, these phrasings and considerations of what is primary and what is secondary in understanding queer Jewish experiences are often a matter of perspective, both from within and outside of that lifeworld. But even the most complex and multifaceted object, regardless of the angle it's viewed from, is nonetheless a singular vessel containing all the multitudes within it. In fact, it is this notion of a complex vessel that returns us to a discussion which we touched upon in the position statement of this book.

The Old Jewish (and Queer) Body

Jamaica: First of all, I had to deal with the fact that I was mixed race. Then I had to, then I sort of had to figure out where I stood on my faith. And then only after those things had really been settled did I even come to touch the like Sleeping Dragon that was my sexuality.

Elite: The only time that I sort of started questioning gay[ness] in Judaism and or gay[ness] full stop was just when we had the plebiscite. That was a bit of a difficult time because [. . .] all of a sudden all these hateful messages were out in the public sphere and I [. . .] didn't really realize that so many people felt this way. And it was so [. . .] in your face and on your Facebook feed. And so [. . .] a subset of that I guess was how did Jews, how does my own community, feel about [. . .] my sexuality. And obviously there is a subset of Jews that think it's not that cool. And then there's another subset in my mind that feel like it's not ideal but will tolerate it within certain constraints. And then there's probably a third tier of people who are just like "be who you want to be and we'll support you 100 percent". I don't know what the quantum of each of those is. But it didn't really occur to me to think about those things until the plebiscite because it sort of bought it all to the fore in a very sort of aggressive way.

As discussed in the position statement of this book, the landscape of Jewish life post-World War II brought with it this notion of the *new Jewish body* [2]. This physical and metaphysical reconceptualization of the so-called "Jewish body" was formed in direct contrast to what was perceived to be the kind of embodiment which landed the Jews in strife time and time again – a weak, effeminate, and highly "abnormal" way of being which supposedly made us susceptible to hostility. Here we already see a remarkable link between Jewishness and queerness, one that extends through centuries and reveals much more about the colonial and cis-heterosexist worldview than it does the material lived reality of Jews and queers. We see what is valued (physical strength and conformity) and what is abhorred (sissyness and oddity). In fact it was not that long ago that the word "Jew" was considered as much a description of queerness as it was of an actual Jewish person [3]. These categories share a common ancestry in the social imaginary and have been entangled with one another particularly in the eyes of those who despise both Jews and queers [4].

The conflation of Jewishness and queerness over the centuries has formed a mechanism which serves myriad purposes. Arguably its most significant outcome is a kind of collective gaslighting of both queer and Jewish people; by framing queers and Jews as having dispositions or natural inclinations towards signifiers of weakness and outsiderness, both groups have been seemingly doomed to a life of violence and exclusion. Antisemitism and homophobia have been situated as life factors which are unavoidable, and pathways towards uprooting these issues are positioned as either impossible or highly improbable [5, 6]. As such, queers and Jews have been told that this is the "way of the world" – both in terms of these groups' stereotyped ways of existing and the inevitable societal backlash. In response to this we have seen a kind of rubber band effect, with significant portions of both populations becoming increasingly obsessed with strength, muscularity, and conformity as pushback against characterizations of frailty or proneness to victimization [7, 8]. It is vital to note that these reactions are not simply cultural responses but are often initiated by traumatic events – masculinized body ideals have been directly connected to both the *Shoah* and the AIDS crisis, with muscularity providing a counterpoint to the "weakness" inflicted upon those peoples [9, 10]. However, as discussed in earlier chapters, while this response is understandable and arguably successful in its most primitive sense, capitulating to these normative conceptions of physical strength as the key to group endurance requires a significant denial of that group's complex history.

We have to ask ourselves: what is left behind when queers and Jews prioritize an aggressive, hypermasculine conception of survival (i.e. the Muscle Jew), and at what point does this focus begin to take away crucial parts of those peoples' queerness and Jewishness? Whether we are looking at the ways in which Jewish muscularity has divorced Jews from their fellow inhabitants in Palestine [11], or the homonegative effects resulting from the proliferation of the notion of "straight-acting" gay people [12], it is obvious that separation from aspects of queerness and Jewishness which have been deemed "victimizable" only leads us down an ever-narrowing path. That is to say, our road to queer and Jewish liberation, autonomy, and thriving is not a singular route, formed in concrete and lined up perfectly towards a goal; rather it is a soft path carved and re-carved by intrigued travellers seeking to explore, to create desire lines through the lush greenery which has been planted and tended to by countless ancestors, and to relish in the very existence of the path itself.

The rejection borne of these external forces does not only cause conflict between queers or Jews and the broader world but also between these marginalized groups themselves. Antisemitism continues to hold a covert but undeniable place in many LGBT+ communities

Shosh: you mentioned that you had experiences of anti-Semitism growing up. Have you had more recent experiences as well, that are sort of reiterating that feeling?

Dahni: No other than just the general "vibe" in society. And so also being mindful sometimes about [that]. [. . .] Because it's part of my identity that I can hide, I won't talk about things or I'll try to avoid certain topics of conversation.

[13], and homophobia and transphobia remain rife within many Jewish spaces [14]. The irony is of course that at the very core of these collectivizing hatreds lies a set of issues which Jews and queers consistently share. The inability of many of us to "pass" or fully embody normative western ideals, and therefore our ability to fully ensure our safety in a white, cisheterosexist world, is something which people within these groups (and of course those of us who belong to both) share [15]. Both Jewishness and queerness pose a threat to Western notions of gender roles, binaries, beauty standards, relationship structures, productivity, and so on. Even those of us who are able to seemingly conform seamlessly with the rigid structures of these societal norms are always living on borrowed time; you can only present as a person without a past, a culture, a voice[1], or a non-conforming body for so long before something shines a light on those aspects of oneself which set you apart from what is considered correct and appropriate.

Here I'd like to return to a notion I discussed in the position statement of this book – *corpulence*. Although I initially explored this concept in the form of *corpulent Judaism*, a contrast point to the *muscular Judaism* described by Presner [2], we can see how this idea extends into the realm of queerness. Beginning with queer peoples' actual bodies, we see how normativity and homophobic/transphobic violence foists on us the kind of compulsive bodily control which produces eating disorders [17] and body dysmorphia [18]. In our attempts to conform, to become small enough so as to be unnoticeable, we inflict harm on our bodies that has significant consequences for our physical health [19]. If the tension and intense discipline inherent to notions of (white) muscularity, "straight-acting", and "cis-passing" are broken in any way, we risk being perceived as aligning with elements which are in direct opposition to a good society [20].

Ariel: I wonder if [. . .] I presented differently, if I had a different body type . . . Coz I really love carbs, so I've got huge-ass boobs and a huge-ass butt, and big ol' hips. If I had you know, if I had different looking hair or, you know, if I was like really tiny and had no curves or if I had short hair or if I dressed in a slightly more androgynous way . . . Whether or not people would even, would maybe take me a little bit more seriously.

It's important to consider that there are many instances of excess which Western societal norms uphold as *good excess*: if you are a person with a large amount of wealth, have many possessions and properties, maintain a schedule that is full to the brim, and have many biological children within a monogamous marriage, you are likely celebrated by the majority of people[2]. But take away any of

---

1 Both figuratively and literally [16].
2 Think of the Kardashians, or the Brady Bunch, depending on your media preference.

those excesses, or replace them with other types, and you can easily become someone with *bad excess*: too many lovers, too much spare time, too many "fur babies", too much body hair or tattoos or fat or anything else which has been deemed as requiring curtailing or so-called moderation. It is this place of *bad excess*, of *corpulence*, where many Jewish and queer experiences meet. We are too loud, sexually ambiguous, difficult to gender – our existence tends to spill over the edges of whatever container the broader societies we live within attempt to fit us into.

Many of these supposed excesses are also artefacts of our histories and the ways Jews and queers have been positioned in contrast to "good society". That is to say, both Jews and queers have been a force of resistance and challenge to the metrics of goodness set up by the dominating forces of wherever we find ourselves. The archetype of Jews as hoarders of money and knowledge was created through European societies' sequestering of Jews to these limited areas of work, largely due to various doctrines of Catholicism and other Christian faiths [21–23]. Similarly, archetypes of queer excess, in particular around practices such as public and intergenerational sex, have their roots in how queer sex (particularly between men) has been regulated and regimented by heterosexuals both historically and in more modern eras such as the AIDS crisis [24, 25]. What is deemed appropriate or excessive, or in other words what we have been led to believe is either *good* or *bad*, is therefore much more a product of historical bigotry and segregation than a reflection of a platonic ideal of human existence.

If society's attempts at erasing our differences, at making our uniquities so anaemic that they simply shrivel away, is part of a movement towards creating new Jewish (and queer) bodies [2], then

Slam: I love identifying as bisexual now, as well as a lesbian, as well as a faggot.

one of our most powerful tools of resistance is the reclamation of *Old Bodies*. That is to say, society demands of Jews and queers a particular way of existing that is, in essence, a simulacra of the ways our oppressors exist; in order to resist it, we must break away from any illusion of sameness, of approximation to dominant culture as a pathway to liberation. This is less a matter of traditionalism or conservativism and more an investigation of what it is about our lived experiences as Jews and queers that has been suppressed, erased, or otherwise opposed. We also need to consider why it is that these aspects of our existence are met with such ire; what threats do Jewishness and queerness carry to the status quo?

When I invoke this notion of *Old Bodies*, it carries with it multiple meanings. I am referring first and foremost to the embodiments of queerness and

Margie: I was very attracted to the Kabbalistic side, the spiritual side of Judaism and the renewal movement. [. . .]. So when I found out about that, that really resonated with me because I had, as a [. . .] university age person being into Zen Buddhism and general Ascetic things. So the spirituality was something that I really longed for. And then [I] found out [. . .] that because of the Holocaust Jews [. . .] kind of had to give up on spirituality because they were getting killed.

Jewishness that have been and continue to be denigrated: bodies which have undergone ritualistic or otherwise affirming modifications (e.g. circumcision, genital reconstruction surgery); bodies which are misaligned with beauty ideals both historical and contemporary (e.g. hairiness, non-conforming gendered mannerisms or dress); bodies which connect in ways that are taboo (e.g. tribadism); bodies which are literally older, more disabled, or otherwise ill-fitting within both physical and figurative structures of society. But I am also referring to *Old Bodies* in a way that is not dissimilar to Lovecraft's Great Old Ones – horrors that are beyond explanation, outside the realm of human language and comprehension [26]. Yes, Lovecraft in many ways was attempting to describe his fear of Jews and queers (and other marginalized groups) by invoking these ancient monstrosities [27], but in doing so he also provides a significant lesson in the power of these supposed outside entities. The Great Old Ones are not simply a thing to be reviled or battled against, but they are also feared for their capacity to upheave the world as we know it [28].

I've written elsewhere about how queer theory (amongst other disciplines) has harnessed monstrosity as a positive descriptor of queer and trans experiences [29], and I would argue the same is true for Jewishness. Jewish traditions of mysticism and theology hold many truths and practices which cut to the core of human existence, including aspects of our life which are uncomfortable or difficult to comprehend. You need to look no further than the writings in the Sefer Yetzirah [30] or the Zohar [31] to realize that Jewish traditions are capable of opening gateways which radically shift one's perspective of the material world. We may not be personally able to create a Golem, or enter and leave Paradise unscathed, but within these tales are descriptions of relationships between people and the cosmos which ameliorate normative constructions of an anthropocentric universe.

What is more threatening to white supremacy and Christian doctrines than a culture or faith which espouses our capacity to directly intermingle with the Divine through personal and communal practices [32, 33]? This is not simply the Divine in the sense of a singular G-d, but Divinity in its ultimate unknowability. In Kabbalah[3], we climb up the Tree of Life, the ten knowable qualities of G-d [34], only to bump our heads repeatedly against the forever unknowable *Keter* (Crown) – the place only that which is Divine in itself can access. There are intersections here with concepts such as Muñoz's queer horizontality and futurity [35], wherein the nature of queerness is that of indefinite extension towards a place we will never fully arrive at. These conceptualizations of human existence as that which is ultimately ever-expanding and never-fully-comprehensible are just one example of the powerful knowledges embedded within these ways of being. They are also examples of the kind of danger queer and Jewish existence poses to normative societal structure, specifically those which seek to replace questions and wonderings with answers and conclusions.

These challenges inevitably find themselves embedded in our physical as well as collective bodies. Whether in moments of mourning or celebration, ecstasy or doom, in solitude or mass gatherings, we are able to invoke the *Old Bodies* and their ways. Queer and Jewish methods of engagement with our selves as well as our kin have a (meta)physicality that is both undeniable and impossible to fully comprehend. These are invoked through ritual, prayer, rest, fucking, celebration, and the myriad other ways we open a gateway between ourselves and others, ourselves and our multitudinous selves, ourselves and the

> *Shosh*: where does Jewishness sit with your life now?
> *Margie*: Basically in every cell of my body. I mean it always was because you can't really get away from it. No, you can't escape. Well, some people can, but I definitely couldn't, you know [. . .] I heard the Holocaust stories, I read everything on the Holocaust before I was 10. I couldn't get away from it and, and it's influenced me totally.

Divine. This is where the true impact of the nexus between Jewishness and queerness is perhaps most noticeable; in using our selves to penetrate membranes that have been rigidly defined by the broader systems around us, in *corpulently* spilling beyond the vessel of Christian, heterosexual, cisgender existence, we show that there are other worlds which can be explored.

Maps and Vessels, Otherness and Elsewhereness

Normative Western world structures would have you believe a myriad of supposed "truths": that each day must be dedicated to productivity [36]; that

---

3 A Jewish mystical practice.

Elsa: I mean, growing up . . .
I think [being] Jewish was the
first thing that I noticed before
being a Person of Colour, like
I noticed that I was Jewish and
everyone else wasn't. At school,
like when we would do RE (religious education) or something
I'd be cordoned off to a separate
room with the other Jews and
Muslim kids. [. . .] There's like
four of us who are all colouring,
you know, while all the other
kids do their Christian religious
education. [Also] at Christmas
time or Easter time, whenever
there was a holiday and, you
know, going to art class and
everyone else is colouring in
an Easter bunny and you get a
star to colour in or something
like that. I think a lot of those
things you feel a lot when you're
a kid because you do just kind
of want to be like everyone else.
You have a really keen sense
of justice as a kid as well, you
know, and it's [. . .] not informed
by intersectional politics,
or like . . .

Shosh: [It's] quite personal.

Elsa: It's so personal. And you're
[wondering] why are all those
kids colouring one thing, and
I have to colour in something
else, you know? But it's so acute
at the same time. And it's amazing that a kid can identify that,
and yet no one else seems to
think that that's an issue.

sexuality is a finite set of behaviours which can only happen between certain types of people [37]; that certain body parts, clothing, mannerisms, and ways of socializing dictate one's personhood [38]; that even something as incomprehensible as Divinity can be whit-tled down to a step-by-step Hero's Journey [39]. However, even the most assimilated and normatively aligned queer or Jewish person cannot help but exceed these seemingly iron-clad boundaries. Even if we work our hardest to suppress every desire, every cultural aspect, and every hint of our so-called *otherness*, we cannot help but leak outside the boundaries of the vessel of normativity.

When we discuss *otherness* we might imag-ine a town map. In the centre is where all the common activities of the town take place, such as commerce and education, child-rearing, and so on. Each building is named on this map, and the paths and other points of connection between these buildings are laid out in fine detail. By contrast, the outskirts are depicted as darkened corners, with specifics and finer points slowly fading into obscurity. Finally, the map simply ends, whether by fading into obscurity or through indicating that beyond the edges of the map lie monsters or other forces which will not allow one to travel safely or at all [40].

This is how we have come to understand social otherness, viewing its residents as shad-ows who creep in from beyond the edges of what is known (or should be known). But both Jews and queers know the true nature of shad-ows; for centuries the core elements which make up these aspects of ourselves have undergone intentional and systematic processes of reduction, of darkening, of disfigurement. But to no avail. We have been made into physical shadows of our former selves, either through state-sanctioned torture or ostracization, and yet survived as peoples. Our teachings and relationships have been forced into darkness, lit only by candlelight or the dim bulbs of attics, city limit bars, or other places of refuge – and yet our ways of life persist. In many ways a shadow is only a shadow to those who value the supposed empirical truth brought on by light. But many things can be learned in the dark.

Mapmaking as a colonial practice is always contingent on two principles: boundaries and centres. By its nature this two-dimensional perspective on the world requires these elements in order to exist, or else it becomes something else entirely. A map must begin and end somewhere, and draw focal points in areas which the mapmakers deem most important. The streets and buildings detailed in the aforementioned town map are no more vital to the existence of the map than the town's seemingly treacherous or unknown surroundings, but their affect is significantly different. The natural architecture surrounding this man-made set of structures is often relegated to lines and gradations of colour, except where a place is deemed especially useful or dangerous to the inhabitants of that town. Through this lens we can see how Western and colonial efforts in mapmaking (both topographical and sociological) inevitably require demonization or minimization of certain parts of a place in order to establish the importance of others. After all, a map which is just as detailed in labelling each stone formation, tree, and nook in a body of water soon ceases to be a map that is deemed useful. Mapmaking requires loss of identity for some aspects in order to ascribe greater meaning to others – this is the root of that *otherness* which both Jews and queers have long contended with.

But the world is not two-dimensional[4], no matter what the mapmakers say. If we return to the notion of *corpulence*, of leaking and spilling over the edges of what is dictated to us by proponents of hegemony, this reality becomes even clearer. Marginalized peoples do not simply huddle together at the corners of maps, where mapmakers can still clearly identify where we reside. We are not living in a place that is *other* to the town centre; we live *elsewhere*. When a vessel overflows, its contents must go somewhere[5]. In that act

Hunter: There is an extent to which [white/non-Jewish people's] attitude to knowledge and their attitude to learning is very different to the attitude that I was taught at [Jewish] school and the attitude I was taught at home, which is [that] you're constantly learning. That's just something that you do, you go into the world curious. You're not doing knowledge for BCE or for year 12 or university. You're doing it because it's what you do. So [I have] that kind of seeking of knowledge.

4   In fact arguably it is much closer to having 10 or 11 dimensions [41].
5   Usually on the white shirt I decided to wear that day.

of overflowing, the vessel is revealed for what it is; just one boundaried container existing in a much larger world. This larger world contains that sense of *elsewhereness* that we have been duped into mistaking for *otherness*. When someone is an *other* to a particular system or space, they exist in relation to those elements in perpetuity. But when we understand that we exist *elsewhere*, it becomes clearer that those restrictive spaces are just as *other* to us as we are to them. It allows us to understand our uniquities not as aberrations but as entirely different worlds. This reminds me of a joke:

> A Jewish man dies and goes to Heaven. When he arrives, an Angel takes him on a tour of the place. After walking around for some time he encounters an old friend of his who passed away a few years back. "But he is a Muslim! How come we are in the same place?" he asks. The Angel replies "all people go to the same place after death". They continue walking, and the man suddenly stops and exclaims "is that Max? My childhood dog?" The Angel replies "yes, all living beings go to the same place after death". They continue walking when the man notices a gigantic concrete wall. "What's behind there?" the man asks. The Angel replies "oh that's where we keep the Evangelicals, that way they think they're the only ones here."[6]

In other words, when we recognize our *elsewhereness*, we are liberating ourselves from these dogmatic walls which falsely delineate who or what is good, worthy, and sacred. We can see these narrow views for the acts of self-oppression that they are, as well as gaining a deeper understanding of the ways our own existences have been suppressed and cajoled into conformity. Yes, there are material realities which cannot be ignored; we *are* pushed into the margins of places and societies. We *are* shunned, or only allow access to the crucial resources within the "city limits" under strict rules. We continue to be harassed, vilified, and killed for who we are[7]. It is in many ways our burden to bear as landless peoples, both Jews and queers. As long as the laws and cultures of the lands we find ourselves in fail to extinguish antisemitism, homophobia, and transphobia, we remain vulnerable. However, I have to make it clear that this *elsewhere* I have been discussing does not imply that we must live separately, either geographically or culturally, from the rest of the world. Whether you are looking at the impact of the creation of the "Jewish state" of Israel on Palestinians or how movements such as Lesbian Separatism have amplified anti-trans sentiments among queers [44], it is obvious that one of the core antecedents of exclusion, discrimination, and persecution is less about that

---

6 Credit to Katherine Jayne Thorpe for introducing me to this wonderful joke.
7 Especially in places with easier civilian access to lethal weapons [42, 43].

one particular vessel we have been discussing (heterosexuality, Christianity, and so on), and more a matter of creating any restrictive vessel to begin with.

In fact, coming to terms with the *elsewhereness* of queerness and Jewishness is a process that is diametrically opposed to the rigidity of walls and borders. In understanding that there is always an *elsewhere* we can come to understand the permeability of many of the socially constructed membranes we have often been instructed to view as concrete. If we continue with the metaphor of the vessel, then we can see that this vessel is resting on a surface, with many potential objects surrounding it. Each object may hold its own set of boundaries, but they are all in proximity (and often contact) with one another. In some ways this is an extension of Sara Ahmed's [45] discussion of how a table might carry with it a set of relational convergences and contradictions: how we define the vessels, and the surface upon which they rest, can either obscure or highlight their interwoven connections. It would be folly to think that a collection of objects resting on a surface have no relationship, do not exist in some kind of complimentary fashion to one

Madelaine: Obviously I'm white but some of those cultural WASPy uptight norms I don't quite get. You know my partner's . . . You know I spend time with her family and her father was a Uniting Church minister and they're not super religious at all but they're very WASP and very shut down and they've got that very Protestant work ethic and they're very repressed in that way. And my partner comes to family dinners and it's loud and it's aggressive in ways and [. . .] we talk about things [more] and there's more food, and there's all those things that I think are an important part of my cultural identity that I don't necessarily talk a lot about but I do feel it. And that's probably why I go to synagogue as well it's like, I feel that separation of myself from general white Protestant Australian culture and it's attached to my Judaism and also my queerness.

another, or at the very least produce meaning through their proximity and positioning to one another. The vessel of cishetero Christianity, then, is not merely something which we have all been poured into only to eventually spill out of. It *is* a part of our collective lived experience, no matter how far away we get from it. But its importance and vitality are only as dominant as we allow them to be; there are multitudes of other choices to be made.

All things eventually meet in some way or another, either by cooperation or counterpoint. In a sense, both Jews and queers highlight the blended edges and points of intersection between supposedly siloed ways of existing. After all, both groups exist in practically every nation, regardless of that nation's attitude towards them. Jews have found themselves everywhere in the world, ironically as a result of being driven out of so many places by pogroms and other types

Dahni: [That's] the thing about the concept of intersectionality, and the [idea of]competing identities. I think the[re is an] idea of intersectionality [which] is that one of your identities has to take primacy, which is problematic because it's not the way we actually function as people. Different parts of my identity will be more important at different points in time depending on what I'm experiencing or what I'm doing.

of anti-Semitic violence [46]. Similarly, queer people continue to be born in every part of the earth where human beings are born, no matter how homophobic or transphobic that place is. Projects such as Queering the Map [47] extend this truth beyond simply a matter of "queer existence" in so-called Australia; the project provides an interactive map which is a living archive of queer experiences across Australia, each memory or anecdote "pinned" to the map by individuals who had queer experiences in this particular location. Similarly, publications such as Growing Up Queer in Australia[8] [48] have shown that queer (and specifically queer Jewish) experiences in Australia are vibrant, diverse, and, most importantly, thriving despite all pressure to disappear or be otherwise silenced. These are not just life signals but documentation of queer joy, pleasure, confusion, distress, and complexity – the fullness of queer Australian life displayed in all its messy details.

Like two particles in a state of quantum entanglement [49], our existence in one place is also inevitably tied to our existence in another. This means that we are always risking rejection; each society or nation can determine that our Jewishness or queerness defies the laws of the land, that our kind belongs to another nation with different moral or legal structures to their own. Despite this, we continue to exist as individuals and as a loose global collective which feels both pain and pleasure as a group. This collective connection, this entanglement, is something that feels both inherently Jewish and queer. As Rebbe Taub states in his discussion of one of The Rebbe's[9] letters [50], Jews may be individual people with extremely diverse experiences and perspectives, but they ultimately form a singular body, meaning all Jews are affected by the actions and experiences of any singular Jew in the world. Similarly, the phrase "none of us are free until we are all free"[51], which originates in Black queer writing, touches on this same notion: all queers are intrinsically tied to the liberation of all other queers, as well as the liberation of all other oppressed peoples. We rejoice at queer triumph as much as we collectively grieve queer suffering

8 Whose publisher unfortunately holds a publicly antagonistic relationship to Palestinian liberation.

9 The title given to Rebbe Menachem Mendel Schneerson, who was considered by many to be a true Tzadik, an enlightened disciple of G-d.

and death. I have experienced an immense sense of pleasure and victory at seeing successful queer Jewish actions such as IfNotNow's campaign against Zionist lobbying [52], and I have wept alongside others when tragedies such as the Pulse shooting transpired [53]. Halfway across the world, these experiences touch me, and for that I am grateful. It is only in connecting myself not only emotionally but metaphysically to those who share my experiences that I can live in a way that is empathetic, compassionate, and, most importantly, enriching to myself and others who share in my struggle for liberation.

Landlessness as Solidarity

The truth is that our existences form a tether between these places; our entanglement is not simply between Jews here and Jews there, or queers in one place with those in another. Rather, we are both producers and carriers of culture who are often responsible for the kinds of cross-pollination which enhances and nourishes the places we find ourselves in. Our *landlessness*, our seemingly increasing ubiquity, means that at the core of our existences is the potential to bring different perspectives and resources to wherever we find ourselves. In our centuries-long experiences of persecution and denial of existence, we are able to link in with others who are also disaffected by the systems which oppress us. This is why there has been such a large movement for solidarity with Aboriginal peoples in Australia amongst both Jews and queers[10] [56, 57]. In some ways what I have been discussing so far is more of an ideal, a framework of Jewish and queer justice that is available to us if we choose to accept it. After all, we live under capitalist colonialism, which has undeniably poisoned us against other marginalized groups in much the same way it has poisoned those groups against us. Nonetheless, I believe it is crucial to discuss the potentialities of solidarity that are inherent to both Jewishness and queerness.

Perhaps the most galvanizing recent example of these roots of solidarity is the COVID-19 pandemic, which is very much ongoing at the time I am writing this. This pandemic has disproportionately affected several marginalized communities, in particular disabled and elderly people as well as Aboriginal peoples in Australia [58–60]. Even if we disregard the fact that many queer and Jewish people are also disabled, elderly, and/or Aboriginal, you can see how queer and Jewish experiences might galvanize those groups into actions of solidarity. After all, who could better understand the impact of mass viral

10 Though this is by no means a blanket rule, as many Jews and queers continue to perpetuate these issues [54, 55].

epidemics and pandemics than queer people [61]? The memory of the AIDS crisis remains living in the bodies of many queer elders and their (biological and cultural) successors. Similarly, who could better understand the outcomes of governmental and systemic mechanisms which deem one group negligible in favour of another's survival? Jews have long been scapegoats and prone to governmental desertion at the first sign of mass public health crises [62]. Both these narratives are woven together through these groups' *landlessness* – by their lack of traditionally understood belonging to a particular place, which often translates to a rejection or sidelining of their needs in favour of those who are considered as belonging to the land.

Jonathan: I definitely don't feel a sense of belonging among the LGBT community most of the time. I usually feel quite alienated at LGBT events.

Ariel: I think when you have a parallel of your own history and you know, if you look at that from an intersectional lens and going, actually, I have a lot of privileges even in my own history compared to being First Nations, being People of Colour… I'm really disgusted by what happened here.

It is important to understand that potentialities of solidarity are different from how solidarity is enacted on the ground: there are many instances of lateral and cross-group violence amongst marginalized peoples, and always have been. I am therefore writing this as much to highlight the ways queers and Jews share a drive for liberation with other groups as I am writing specifically to galvanize other queer Jews to step up to the mantle and accept the responsibility we have to our marginalized kin. There has been an increasing tendency amongst marginalized peoples (queer, Jewish, or otherwise) to attempt to quantify their negative positioning in relation to dominant forces. Some authors have named this phenomenon the "oppression Olympics" [63], and though I find this term to be ultimately more divisive/derisive than useful in the majority of cases[11], it does highlight how easily people and groups can become insulated from others by their specific experiences of suffering at the hands of dominant cultures and structures. Yes, there may be individual cases of a person leveraging their identifiable lived experience (e.g. race, sexuality, gender) as a means of shutting down others' critiques of their participation in acts of marginalization. But more importantly, it is easy to see how marginalized peoples, particularly those who are clustered together in either geographic or digital spaces, may turn what initially could have been walls of protection into walls of exclusion.

---

11 As it is impossible to deny that we are often forced to weaponize our suffering as a means of survival, often at the expense of others' capacity, e.g. limited funding for supporting victims of domestic violence, people living with a disability, etc.

The aforementioned lesbian separatist movement is an excellent example of this issue: lesbians, particularly during and prior to the early 1990s, were an intensely persecuted group of people across multiple nations and continents. This meant lesbians had to close ranks, become choosy of who is aware of their sexuality and ways of living, and construct moats and drawbridges around their personal and collective existence. Lesbian separatism in Australia thrived during the 70s and 80s with many lesbians forming separatist communes in rural locations across the country [64]. This has had aftershocks with ongoing implications for present-day lesbian politics [65]. Inevitably, who could or could not lay claim to the identity of lesbian became a highly contentious issue which left many people outside the lesbian fortress' gates, namely trans peoples and bi+ people [66]. While this may have seemed like a simple act of security enforcement on the part of those inside the walls of lesbianism, it often meant that those outside the walls either had to fight marginalizing forces on their own or galvanize in ways which were considered entirely separate to lesbians. This division persists today, as can be seen with the persistent (and incorrect) correlation between trans womanhood and heterosexuality [67]. If you're too trans to be a lesbian, but too much of a lesbian to fit normative standards of transness, then you will likely find yourself in a somewhat liminal position[12]. This is not just a philosophically liminal position, but a materially unstable experience which directly affects one's chances of survival.

Sally: There's I think a growing bridge between I'll say the privileged cisgender gay men and some privileged cisgender lesbians compared to almost "the rest". And this opened out during the postal survey that we saw some people, some so-called "rainbow leaders" sell out a lot of people, particularly trans, to some extent bi ... Going beyond me, I believe there are many intersex people who are dissatisfied, and rainbow People of Colour. And I'm still finding that there are lots of good people at the grassroots who are empathic, who do good our leadership to groups they don't identify with, but I feel we have a lot of people in positions of prominence and influence within our "rainbow community" and some of the organizations they're in who are not adapting. Well, they haven't adapted beyond 1980s when it was all cis gay male.

There's still incredible misogyny broadly from some of those organizations and high up people. And that's been a struggle personally. And I have had to question where I fit in. I know I have lots of skills but I don't like hierarchy. I suppose I have ended up over a long period going higher in whatever structure there is. But the higher one goes there's more conservatism, there's more misogynism, transphobia, biphobia ...

12 A "no man's land" if you will.

Living as a butch trans lesbian has meant I have been subject to the substantive effects these lines of division, these *refusals of solidarity*, produce. Lovers, friends, co-workers, and others who have interacted with me over the years seemed moved almost by an invisible hand to deny certain aspects of my existence in order to simplify how they narrativize my existence in their minds. I've been the exception to people's rules of sexuality, whether it is gay men who find me attractive despite my womanhood or lesbians who simply ignore parts of my body that do not fit their personal narrative of their sexuality. My butchness and dykeness have been given such prominence that many people are unsure "what kind of trans" I am[13]. The focus on whether I have a cunt or a cock is at times overwhelming, especially in environments where those factors are completely irrelevant. None of these pressures would exist if we lived in a world which was not obsessed with separating sex, sexuality, and gender and subjugating those who defy the rules of those categories. If queers, Jews, and other groups (which I may or may not belong to) had not been forced to reinforce their barricades as a means of survival, we would not see so many people desperately attempting to avoid persecution by knocking on every castle gate hoping to meet its entry requirements.

I do not want to mislead readers by overusing the metaphor of fortresses and castles when discussing marginalized peoples' isolation, self-inflicted or otherwise. The reality is that most of us, even those who have some ancestral or legally affirmed access to land or other physical spaces, experience some level of displacement and dispossession. This is why the notion of queer and Jewish *landlessness* is such an important aspect of marginalization and solidarity. *Landlessness* exists in opposition to the colonial concept of *landedness*, itself a separate framework of connection to country to that of *indigeneity* [68]. Landedness is about possession, iron-fisted control, and invasion of space, whereas indigeneity encircles around a people's responsibility and mutual relationship with the land and its flora and fauna. Landlessness, by contrast, is a recognition of those groups for whom there is no formal and continuing ownership or belonging to a land, forceful or ancestral. In understanding queers and Jews as landless people, we can unravel some of their specific vulnerabilities, as well as advantages.

In being landless, one might feel compelled to attach to notions of nationalism and patriotism as a means of securing their safety. Certainly as an immigrant to this country, I have felt the pressure to assimilate to "Australian life",

13 I am asked this often.

both in terms of suppressing my racial and cultural background as well as other "un-Australian" aspects of myself such as my sexuality and gender. There was, and still is, little space for a weird Jewish poofter in the rigid edicts of white Australian life. My drive to assimilate was particularly prevalent for the several years between emigrating here and achieving my citizenship, wherein my ability to remain in Australia was in perpetual limbo. Leaving the house meant knowing what gets left at home: no speaking Hebrew in public, avoiding drawing attention to myself, being exceptionally courteous and amiable to people I perceived as powers of authority. These are the main affects which landedness (or striving towards it) produces: fear and desperation to conform. But through engagement with Blak peoples and Blak politics, as well as meditation on my own relationship to the force required to

Margie: My parents loved Australia, loved the bush, because it was the place that took them in, you know, finally. And they could stay, so why would I not [also love Australia]? The other thing is that I feel so strongly about Aboriginal land and Aboriginal people and the Country and all that sort of connection that I just think what a privilege. You know what I mean, apart from politics being completely [bad], I feel grateful to be here. I feel really good that I'm not in Israel,

Shosh: Yeah, it's a tough place.

Margie: Oh yeah.

maintain landedness, I was able to find comfort and power in my landlessness. I have no legitimate ancestral claim to so-called Australia in much the same way as I have no claim to so-called Israel; my ancestors never visited the former and were banished centuries ago from the latter, only to return through a twisted web of post-World War II bureaucracy and antisemitism. Though my body will be returned to the (most likely Australian) soil, this soil is not where this body was formed. The same is true for Israeli soil; I am merely the second generation in my family to be born on those lands. My ancestral ties are myriad, and therefore their concentration in my body is not so easily distinguishable. I do not owe my existence to any singular piece of land.

This, however, does not mean that I can shirk responsibility for the lands I currently occupy. Landlessness can be a tool and has certainly played a part historically in Jewish resistance to colonization and the formation of nation-states [69]. Jewish existence, in its *elsewhereness* and *landlessness*, sticks in the craw of powers who seek to flatten lands and peoples into homogenous singularity. The same is true of queer landlessness: there is no geographic or genetic fountainhead from which queerness flows, and to which queer people can be banished. Therefore, our existence in any given place can form a stronghold of resistance to assimilation, to those seeking to narrow our lives into uniformity or unassailable binaries. What this means in practice varies from place to place, but in the geopolitical context of this research, there are some clear pathways for using one's *landlessness* in pursuit of justice and solidarity.

Firstly, there must be an acknowledgement of how important land is, particularly for Traditional Owners and the peoples of that land, *especially* those peoples who have been denied access to that land by colonization. Though non-Aboriginal Jews and queers do not have the deep ancestral ties to "Australian" lands that our Aboriginal comrades do, that does not absolve us from recognizing what the land we live on gives us and what we therefore must give to it. In practice, this means that we as landless peoples must support the sovereignty and liberation of Aboriginal peoples across "Australia", including efforts to remove colonial rule from their land [70] as well as excising discriminatory policies and government organizations (e.g. the Australian police force) which perpetuate state violence against those peoples [71–73]. While this matter has been a prominent aspect of solidarity work with Aboriginal peoples for decades, more recent global movements such as Black Lives Matter have further highlighted the need for non-Aboriginal peoples to support the struggle for Blak freedom in Australia [74].

Jewish and queer lives are inextricably linked with these efforts in a number of ways. We too are subject to state violence, though its mechanisms have become less overt in recent years. For example, one might be tempted to see police or police-like presence in synagogues and LGBT spaces as an indication that we are protected by state forces, that the governing institutions are aligned with Jews and queers systematically through these practices of "police allyship". At first blush this might seem to make queers and Jews distinct from Aboriginal peoples, who are intensively and openly targeted by Australian police [75]. However, nothing could be further from the truth; police in Australia and elsewhere continue to enact anti-queer violence [76, 77], and protection of Jewish communities from legitimate hate crimes remains mired by bureaucratic incompetence[14] [78]. There is a reason why Jewish communities are so insular, and why so many queers form tight-knit circles; the reason is that we are in states of collective siege from the violence of state actors such as the police. Many of us have been swayed, no doubt by our fear of other types of violence, into believing the propaganda around the supposed safety provided to our communities by the police.

The most privileged among us are only able to maintain a pro-police (and therefore fundamentally anti-Blak) stance by distancing themselves from the

---

14 If I were to be cynical, I might even suggest that this incompetence is less accidental than it seems.

experiences of our neighbours and comrades, and this position is brittle at best. You can only live for so long, or in such intensive insularity, before you are forced to face the reality that a system which allows violence against one group is ripe for turning itself against another. Engaging with one's landlessness in this instance is therefore an act of empathy, of understanding that even though you do not belong to a piece of land in a traditional sense, you are subject to the politics of the nation-state which holds the land in its grasp. Even if we are currently spared the ire of the state's violent efforts, we need only look upwards

Shosh: So do you feel the need to avoid disclosing [your Jewishness or queerness]? *Elite:* Sometimes I do. To be honest, I guess because you don't know how people will receive the information. And until you feel safe that It's not going to go down badly, whether it's gay or Jewish, then I just would prefer to just not have those discussions and just test those waters.

at the Sword of Damocles to understand that systemic inhumanity is rarely narrow in its focus. In a way this position reflects the issues that have arisen with discourse around the Holocaust, which has effectively erased the Holocaust's impact on non-Jewish groups such as the Romani [79]. But the Holocaust was not merely a Jewish experience: it was a fascist, colonial experience, reflective of many contemporary regimes which work to marginalize and eliminate people based on certain characteristics [80]. To see past this hegemonic perspective on both historical and contemporary events allows us to understand that policies of fascism and targeted state suppression can never benefit humanity as a whole, no matter how small a sliver of society they are currently taking aim at.

It is also important to remind ourselves that in the not-too-distant past both Jews and queers in Australia have been subject to discriminatory and violent government mechanisms and policies, including (but not limited to) the White Australia Policy [81] and both federal and state-based anti-sodomy laws [82]. The vestigial tails of these policies continue to play out in areas such as refugee policies, which continue to restrict access to asylum-seeking in Australia based on sexuality, gender, race, and religious affiliation [83–85]. Here we can see further entanglement between queer and Jewish *landlessness* and the struggles of other marginalized peoples. Not only are our struggles interconnected with the peoples whose lands we live on but also with those peoples fleeing their own lands due to persecution. While Jewish landlessness is largely a historical matter, and queer landlessness can be understood as having a type of non-ancestral ontology[15], the landlessness of refugees is a matter of current

---

15   In that it is not inherited through genetics or biological family lines.

geopolitical conflict, colonization, and genocidal persecution. It is an action, a process of people being removed from their land entirely, often literally forced away from physical land and onto boats or other means of intercontinental escape. This is not to mention that many Jews in Australia are descendants of refugees, myself included. No matter how far any individual Jew or queer person has come in terms of their acceptability within current societal structures, no matter how privileged their personal and familial history, they will always be a potential subject to state violence.

Beyond Queerness and Jewishness

In many ways, this acknowledgement of solidarity, borne of both shared experiences and a larger lens of empathetic action, makes it somewhat difficult to simply discuss how queerness and Jewishness intersect. At the very least, in witnessing the permeability of boundaries around what is Jewish and what is queer, I feel compelled to reach out further than the restraints of the subject of this book. There are many intriguing coincidences and sociohistorical convergences between these experiences, and a significant portion of people who inhabit both categories. But these are not the only categories that my interviewees (and other queer Jews) exist within and across. There are multiple streams of Judaism across an entire globe, and countless ways of identifying one's queer sexuality or transness. Even these subcategories are contextual, and reliant on other points of identity and lived experience. The particles which come to form a single person are comprised of millions of genes, both expressed and suppressed. Whether something within us is illuminated or covered in shadow makes as much of a difference as whether something is present or absent. This is not an attempt at any kind of homogenizing, Pollyanna claims about how "we are all human". In fact my point is the opposite; that the myriad experiences, contexts, and physicalities which comprise any given person make it impossible to reduce collective experiences down to a tangible narrative.

There are most certainly aspects of this book which may enrage other queer Jews, and seem like the furthest thing from their lived reality. Some might baulk at my assertion that our Jewishness begs of us to forego the state of Israel, give Aboriginal peoples their land back, and resist the "mission creep" [86] of an increasingly militarized police force in Australia. Some might find discussions of the importance of G-d and mysticism in Jewish life to be completely irrelevant, if not offensive. Some may even find their categorical inclusion in this research to be entirely misaligned with how they experience their sexuality, gender, and religious or cultural affiliation. These concerns have been looping in my head on repeat for the four years it has taken me to undertake this research. My mantra throughout the writing process has been "touching feeling", referring to Eve Kosofsky Sedgwick's fantastic book by the same name [87]. I've specifically kept the chapter "Paranoid Reading and Reparative Reading, or, You're So Paranoid, You Probably Think This Essay Is About You" at the front of my mind. It can be scary to delve into these issues, into the oozy in-betweens and borderlands that exist in discussions of both Jewishness and queerness. These are highly politicized categories of human-ity, and these groups have both historical and modern struggles across the world. Within these groups there are also disagreements, conflicts, and areas which are deemed too dangerous to tread. I was already familiar with many of these, but the weight of their presence expanded trifold during the time I have spent writing this book. While I hope I have expressed my perspectives respectfully, albeit assertively, I understand that this book may be a challenge to read for many people, including those who might otherwise consider them-selves aligned with me.

After all, without invoking unnecessary gravitas, many of the issues I dis-cuss are not conceptual or abstract; they are tied to the material reality of my participants. My interviews were all tinged with the spectres of Zionism (regardless of the stances taken), antisemitism, homophobia, and transphobia. I have no doubt that at least some – if not all – of my interviewees felt these ghostly presences too. It is not that long ago that speaking of any of these matters in the kinds of spaces I conducted most of my interviews in (cafes, restaurants, or other public spaces) was a calculated risk that many would or could not take. I have discussed earlier my own history of negotiating which spaces were ok to speak Hebrew in, to be visibly queer and trans in, or to stand out in any way at all. I guarantee you that many of these topics are not spoken of with much more ease in private spaces either. There is a sense of survival at stake, of walking a fine line in one's existence between brevity and self-preservation, and between positions of boldness and compromise. Nearly each one of my interviews had moments of hushed tones as topics such as the Occu-pation, medical transition, or less-than-perfect disclosures of sexuality came up.

In a way, this book did not start with a proposal or an ethics application but rather with the sensation of a large lump in my throat going GULP as I pre-pared to both literally and figuratively amplify those secretive, hushed conver-sations. Any person who has asked me about this research over the last four years was met with statements like "I won't be making any friends with this one". But at some point I had to recognize these spectres, these atmospheric threats, for what they were: subjective apparitions, ghouls which may be tied to reality in some way but are distorted by my own personal fears, concerns, and apprehensions. Yes, this book contains "confronting" opinions and discusses murky lived experiences. But it is not being positioned as a monolith, either of queer and trans Jews in general or of my own opinions and experiences specifically. These are impossible to encapsulate. However, in the next and final chapter, I aim to address some of these considerations, trepidations, and points of contention. This is not so much to allay any one group of readers' concerns but to tie together how the topics discussed throughout this book have formed through my own process. My hope is to leave readers intrigued, challenged, and perhaps more deeply considerate of how bodies, societies, and geopolitics are intrinsically intertwined, for better or for worse.

References

[1] Sirin SR, Fine M. Hyphenated selves: Muslim American youth negotiating identities on the fault lines of global conflict. *Appl Dev Sci* 2007; 11: 151–163.

[2] Presner TS. *Muscular Judaism: The Jewish Body and the Politics of Regeneration.* Routledge, 2007.

[3] Jakobsen JR. Queers are like Jews, aren't they? Analogy and alliance politics. *Queer Theory Jew Quest* 2003; 64–89.

[4] Boyarin D. Freud's baby, Fliess's maybe: Homophobia, anti-Semitism, and the invention of Oedipus. *GLQ J Lesbian Gay Stud* 1995; 2: 115–147.

[5] Levine Daniel J, Fyall R, Benenson J. Talking about antisemitism in MPA classrooms and beyond. *J Public Aff Educ* 2020; 26: 313–335.

[6] Wozolek B. Gaslighting queerness: Schooling as a place of violent assemblages. *J LGBT Youth* 2018; 15: 319–338.

[7] Badenes-Ribera L, Fabris MA, Longobardi C. The relationship between internalized homonegativity and body image concerns in sexual minority men: A meta-analysis. *Psychol Sex* 2018; 9: 251–268.

[8] Reizbaum M. Max Nordau and the generation of Jewish muscle. *Jew Cult Hist* 2003; 6: 130–151.

[9] Amraoui Y. Evolutionary aesthetics and the Hebrew male body: Study of the Zionist metamorphosis of the Jewish masculine body and the birth of the "muscle Jew". *IOSR J Humanit Soc Sci*; 16.

[10] Griffiths S, Jotanovic D, Austen E. Androgen abuse among gay and bisexual men. *Curr Opin Endocrinol Diabetes Obes* 2021; 28: 589–594.

[11] Hotam Y. "Re-orient-ation": Sport and the transformation of the Jewish Body and identity. *Isr Stud* 2015; 20: 53–75.

[12] Sáncahez FJ, Vilain E. "Straight-acting gays": The relationship between masculine consciousness, anti-effeminacy, and negative gay identity. *Arch Sex Behav* 2012; 41: 111–119.

[13] Schlosser LZ, Safran RS, Suson RA, et al. Chapter 18 – The assessment, diagnosis, and treatment of mental disorders among American Jews. In: Paniagua FA, Yamada A-M (eds). *Handbook of Multicultural Mental Health (Second Edition)*. San Diego: Academic Press, pp. 347–366.

[14] Brettschneider M. *Jewish Feminism and Intersectionality*. SUNY Press, 2016.

[15] Crasnow SJ. "I Want to Look Transgender": Anti-assimilation, gender self-determination, and confronting white supremacy in the creation of a just Judaism. *J Am Acad Relig* 2020; 88: 1026–1048.

[16] Pennington S. Transgender passing guides and the vocal performance of gender and sexuality. *The Oxford Handbook of Music and Queerness*. Epub ahead of print 11 April 2022. DOI: 10.1093/oxfordhb/9780199793525.013.65.

[17] Parker LL, Harriger JA. Eating disorders and disordered eating behaviors in the LGBT population: A review of the literature. *J Eat Disord* 2020; 8: 1–20.

[18] Deshane E. The other side of the mirror: Eating disorder treatment and gender identity. *LGBTQ POLICY* 2016; 6: 89.

[19] Striegel-Moore RH, Bulik CM. Risk factors for eating disorders. *Am Psychol* 2007; 62: 181.

[20] White FR. Fat, queer, dead: "Obesity" and the death drive. *Somatechnics* 2012; 2: 1–17.

[21] Becker SO, Pascali L. Religion, division of labor, and conflict: Anti-semitism in Germany over 600 Years. *Am Econ Rev* 2019; 109: 1764–1804.

[22] Botticini M, Eckstein Z. *The Chosen Few: How Education Shaped Jewish History, 70–1492*. Princeton University Press. Epub ahead of print 5 August 2012. DOI: 10.1515/9781400842483.

[23] Mell JL. *The Myth of the Medieval Jewish Moneylender*. Springer, <https://link.springer.com/book/10.1057/978-1-137-39778-2> (2017, accessed 11 June 2022).

[24] Foucault M. *The History of Sexuality: The Use of Pleasure*. Vintage Books, 1988.

[25] Mahana M. Still ACTing UP? Voices from ACTUP's oral history project on the current state of the LGBTQ community. *Theses Diss*, <https://academicworks.cuny.edu/hc_sas_etds/317> (2018).

[26] Lovecraft HP. *The Whisperer in Darkness: Collected Short Stories*. Wordsworth Editions, 2007.

[27] Paz CG. Race and war in the Lovecraft Mythos. *Lovecraft Annu* 2012; 6: 3–35.

[28] Bolton K. The Influence of HP Lovecraft on Occultism. *Ir Gothic J* 2011; 9: 2-21.

[29] Rosenberg S. Queer theory and trans people. In: *The SAGE Encyclopedia of Trans Studies*. SAGE Publications Inc, <https://us.sage pub.com/en-us/nam/the-sage-encyclopedia-of-trans-studies/book270824> (2021, accessed 11 June 2022).

[30] Kaplan A. *Sefer Yetzirah: The Book of Creation in Theory and Practice*. Weiser Books, 1997.

[31] Wolfson ER. Light through darkness: The ideal of human perfection in the Zohar. *Harv Theol Rev* 1988; 81: 73–95.

[32] Kaplan A. *Jewish Meditation: A Practical Guide*. Schocken Books, 1985.

[33] Weissler C. Meanings of Shekhinah in the "Jewish Renewal" Movement. *Nashim J Jew Womens Stud Gend Issues* 2005; 53–83.

[34] Besserman P. *The Shambhala Guide to Kabbalah and Jewish Mysticism*. Shambhala Publications, 1998.

[35] Muñoz JE, Chambers-Letson J, Nyong'o T, et al. *Cruising Utopia, 10th Anniversary Edition: The Then and There of Queer Futurity*. NYU Press, 2019.

[36] Tanner K. *Christianity and the New Spirit of Capitalism*. Yale University Press, 2019.

[37] Sehlikoglu S, Karioris FG. *The Everyday Makings of Heteronormativity: Cross-Cultural Explorations of Sex, Gender, and Sexuality*. Rowman & Littlefield, 2019.

[38] Stryker S. *Transgender History: The Roots of Today's Revolution*. Hachette UK, 2017.

[39] Mwai W, Gimode E, Kebaya C. Reading the Story of Jesus Christ as an Epic.

[40] Macfarlane KE. Here be monsters: Imperialism, knowledge and the limits of empire. *Text Matters J Lit Theory Cult* 2016; 74–95.

[41] Antoniadis I, Benakli K. Large dimensions and string physics in future colliders. *Int J Mod Phys A* 2000; 15: 4237–4285.

[42] Vogel-Scibilia S. Community Resilience and the Pittsburgh Synagogue Shooting. In: Moffic HS, Peteet JR, Hankir A, et al. (eds). *Anti-Semitism and Psychiatry: Recognition, Prevention, and Interventions*. Cham: Springer International Publishing, pp. 223–241.

[43] Stults CB, Kupprat SA, Krause KD, et al. Perceptions of safety among LGBTQ people following the 2016 Pulse nightclub shooting. *Psychol Sex Orientat Gend Divers* 2017; 4: 251.

[44] Worthen MG. This is my TERF! Lesbian feminists and the stigmatization of trans women. *Sex Cult* 2022; 26(5): 1–22.

[45] Ahmed S. *Queer Phenomenology: Orientations, Objects, Others*. Duke University Press, 2006.

[46] Aviv CS, Shneer D. *New Jews: The End of the Jewish Diaspora*. NYU Press, 2005.

[47] Queering the Map. Queering the Map, <https://www.queeringthemap.com/>.

[48] Law B. *Growing Up Queer in Australia*. Black Inc., 2019.

[49] Bengtsson I, Życzkowski K. *Geometry of Quantum States: An Introduction to Quantum Entanglement*. Cambridge University Press, 2017.

[50] Taub RS. Rebbe letters: Advice for an extreme introvert on Apple podcasts. *Rebbe Letters*, <https://podcasts.apple.com/au/podcast/advice-for-an-extreme-introvert/id1613985765?i=1000607153895> (2023, accessed 3 August 2023).

[51] Forsgren LDL. Violence, ritual, and vogue: Black queer feminist praxis in motion. *MELUS* 2021; 46: 37–53.

[52] IfNotNow. Our Campaigns. *IfNotNowMovement*, <https://www.ifnotnowmovement.org/our-campaigns> (2023, accessed 3 August 2023).

[53] Ramirez JL, Gonzalez KA, Galupo MP. "Invisible during my own crisis": Responses of LGBT people of color to the Orlando shooting. *J Homosex* 2018; 65: 579–599.

[54] Tatz C. An essay in disappointment: The Aboriginal-Jewish relationship. *Aborig Hist* 2004; 28: 100–121.

[55] Clark M. Indigenous subjectivity in Australia: Are we queer? *J Glob Indig* 2015; 1: 7.

[56] Fischer N. Minor-to-minor intersections: Jewish and Aboriginal Australians between antisemitism and racism. In: *Minor-to-Minor Intersections: Jewish and Aboriginal Australians Between Antisemitism and Racism*. De Gruyter Oldenbourg, pp. 131–148.

[57] Russell EK. *Queer Histories and the Politics of Policing*. Routledge, 2019.

[58] Dudgeon P, Derry K, Arabena K, et al. *A National COVID-19 Pandemic Issues Paper on Mental Health and Wellbeing for Aboriginal and Torres Strait Islander Peoples: Rosenburg, S. (2020) The impact of COVID-19 on mental health – implications for policy and practice in Australia. Croakey, 12 May 2020*. Australia: The University of Western Australia, 2020.

[59] Goggin G, Ellis K. Disability, communication, and life itself in the COVID-19 pandemic. *Health Sociol Rev* 2020; 29: 168–176.

[60] Holt NR, Neumann JT, McNeil JJ, et al. Implications of COVID-19 in an ageing population. *Med J Aust* 2020; 213: 342–344.

[61] Altshuler E. Learning from history: Remembering the successes and failures of the AIDS crisis to fight COVID-19. *Int Public Health J* 2021; 13: 111–117.

[62] Jedwab R, Khan AM, Russ J, et al. Epidemics, pandemics, and social conflict: Lessons from the past and possible scenarios for COVID-19. *World Dev* 2021; 147: 105629.

[63] Hancock A. *Solidarity Politics for Millennials: A Guide to Ending the Oppression Olympics*. Springer, 2011.

[64] Jennings R. Creating feminist culture: Australian rural lesbian-separatist communities in the 1970s and 1980s. *J Womens Hist* 2018; 30: 88–111.

[65] van Aurich A, Hearn K. Lesbian separatism and identity development: Making space for themselves. *Continuum* 2023; 37: 19–30.

[66] Weiss JT. GL vs. BT: The archaeology of biphobia and transphobia within the US gay and lesbian community. *J Bisexuality* 2004; 3: 25–55.

[67] Rossiter H. She's always a woman: Butch lesbian trans women in the lesbian community. *J Lesbian Stud* 2016; 20: 87–96.

[68] Rowe AC, Tuck E. Settler colonialism and cultural studies: Ongoing settlement, cultural production, and resistance. *Cult Stud ↔ Crit Methodol* 2017; 17: 3–13.

[69] Shneer D. *Yiddish and the Creation of Soviet Jewish Culture: 1918–1930*. Cambridge University Press, 2004.

[70] Kuriype R. Recognising indigenous land: Analysing the success of native title and land rights campaigns. *NEW Emerg Sch Aust Indig Stud* 2018; 4: 58–64.

[71] Pennay A, Savic M, Seear K, et al. Decriminalising public drunkenness: Accountability and monitoring needed in the ongoing and evolving management of public intoxication. *Drug Alcohol Rev* 2021; 40: 205–209.

[72] Hart C. Neocolonialism: The true intention behind the Northern Territory intervention. *NEW Emerg Sch Aust Indig Stud* 2018; 4: 76–82.

[73] Liddle C. Australia still turns a blind eye to Aboriginal people dying in police custody. *Chain React* 2021; 12–13.

[74] Schuitenmaker C. Rattling those cages: Reflections on indigenous voices in the Black Lives Matter Movement in Australia. *SEM Stud News* 2022; 17: 1–5.

[75] Green J. The impacts of control, racism, and colonialism on contemporary Aboriginal-police relations. *NEW Emerg Sch Aust Indig Stud*; 5.

[76] Myers KA, Forest KB, Miller SL. Officer friendly and the tough cop: Gays and lesbians navigate homophobia and policing. *J Homosex* 2004; 47: 17–37.

[77] Dwyer A, Bond CEW, Ball M, et al. Support provided by LGBTI police liaison services: An analysis of a survey of LGBTIQ people in Australia. *Police Q* 2022; 25: 33–58.

[78] Vergani M, Link R. A conceptual framework to map responses to hate crime, hate inci-
dents and hate speech: The case of Australia. *Soc Policy Soc* 2021; 1–18.

[79] Richardson KL. Invisible strangers, or romani history reconsidered. *Hist Present* 2020;
10: 187–207.

[80] Moses AD. The German Catechism – Geschichte der Gegenwart. *Geschichte der Gegenwart*, <https://geschichtedergegenwart.ch/the-german-catechism/>.

[81] Creese J. Secular Jewish identity and public religious participation within Australian secular multiculturalism. *Religions* 2019; 10: 69.

[82] Albion A, Russell EK. Governing queer histories and futures: A critical place-based analysis of state apology. *Crit Criminol* 2022; 1–16.

[83] Dawson J. The externalization of Australian refugee policy and the costs for queer asylum
seekers and refugees. *Aust J Int Aff* 2020; 74: 322–339.

[84] Oberman K. Refugee discrimination–the good, the bad, and the pragmatic. *J Appl Philos*
2020; 37: 695–712.

[85] Ziersch A, Due C, Walsh M. Discrimination: A health hazard for people from refugee and
asylum-seeking backgrounds resettled in Australia. *BMC Public Health* 2020; 20: 1–14.

[86] MCCULLOCH J. Welfare to warfare: Police militarisation and Fortress Australia. *AQ
Aust Q* 2021; 92: 3–11.

[87] Sedgwick EK. *Touching Feeling: Affect, Pedagogy, Performativity.* Duke University
Press, 2003.

· 6 ·

BELONGING: THREADS AND DEAD ENDS

This final chapter is focused on how the discussions and theories brought up throughout the book affect queer and trans Jews' experiences of "belonging". The term "belonging" is in itself quite broad, and often contradictory. One might assume belonging to a community is a matter of category, but lived experiences of queer and trans Jewishness in Australia point to a much more complex truth. The impact of Australian colonialism, historical queer and Jewish persecution, and contemporary tensions about the Israel-Palestine "conflict" lead to experiences of belonging which cannot be neatly categorized as either belongingness or a lack thereof. In order to understand how belongingness is created, experienced, and at times destroyed, this chapter will discuss the "threadlessness" of queer and Jewish history, and provide a more detailed exploration of how our relationships with ourselves, with each other, and with the world come together to form complex, uneven, and at times even unrecognizable experiences of "belonging".

Tracing Our Threads

There is a sense of threadlessness about Jewishness, about queerness. A tradition disrupted, a windswept tree growing at such an angle that its *treeness* is barely recognizable. It's that sense of having one's personal and collective experiences outside normative structures relegated to what Andrew E. Benjamin[1] describes as "the fragmentary, the incomplete and the partial" (p. ix). When I say threadlessness, I'm referring to the kind of thread you follow back, the one meant to lead you home from the dark and twisty forest. Where whites and straights have a strong braided rope of tradition (no matter how toxic that tradition is), Jews and queers are often lucky to find even a trace of fabric. We find ourselves wherever fortune has landed us, and our way back to safety is never guaranteed.

This metaphor has stuck with me for the last decade; a throwaway line from my favourite (dead) therapist Steven. We discussed coming out late, and the effect of growing up detached from any sense of community, history, or even personal narrative which includes queerness among its tales. "It's very hard to find the thread", he said, "for some people there is none at all". I was suddenly entranced, realizing the magnitude of it all. What did it mean to have my line to safety and self-understanding shaved down to a single fragile strand? Who is responsible for this? Can a single thread ever become stronger? Where was I now? Where was I heading? Where is home?

Our threads are shaved, burned, and cut in myriad ways. The AIDS crisis ruthlessly severed our ties to a whole generation's worth of history keepers and storytellers, leaving in its wake a queer narrative shrouded in loss [2]. The Holocaust and its pogrom predecessors had radically reduced the scope of Jewish history-keeping[3], forcing a focus on a kind of "guardianship" of sorrow [4], of paranoia, of What Happened and What Must Never Happen Again. And like the burning embers of never-to-be-recovered archives at the Institut für Sexualwissenschaft[5], existing at the intersection of these collective traumas is a process which incinerates matter, flesh, and spirit.

I have been discussing this sense of threadlessness at a collective level, at a historical level. But it is a process embedded in the body. Right now I write with distance and clarity, the kind afforded by surviving past what was expected of me as a self-destructing 20-something. It is also the kind of clarity afforded to me by my privileged status as a person completing a Doctorate, who is able to access the kinds of resources (both academic and otherwise) which have positioned me in this way. It's easy for me to discuss the intersections of trauma and history and peoples, with what I know and feel now. But in a linoleum-covered chair, in that starchy clinic counsellor's office, so close to the waiting room I swore I could hear people wordlessly dreading a positive diagnosis through the wall, I was perplexed. Steven was not speaking of the countless threads of politics and human relationships washing across centuries; he was talking about me.

I once had a coil of thread inside me. Strong, brightly coloured, wrapped around itself like a dozing lover on a frosty morning waiting for you to come back to bed. One end was tied to the foot of my very first bed, and the rest left with me to carry and unspin as I went on existing. At first I left spools of string on the floors of my many childhood homes, crawling and circling and noting each little corner of my small domain. Then, as I became more independent, more and more of this thread was left behind me as I moved, as I grew, as I exited the military zone I called home to move to a place I only vaguely understood.

This coil tied me to myself, led me back to who I was, and where I would eventuate. I often think of the Tralfamadorians from Vonnegut's *Slaughterhouse Five*[6], whose entire personal history physically stretches behind and ahead of them like a worm. They are a child, a teenager, an elderly being, all at once; their thread so seamlessly connected that they already know where they are going, and will always remember where they have gone. Reading that book as a teen, I was jealous of them, and never understood why.

The coil is tied to our destiny, what we think we are, and where we think we will go. In its ideal state, it evenly unfurls as we explore, as we pace. It allows us to see when we have returned to familiar ground, or have simply been treading a circular desire line through the forest. When we find ourselves facing an unknown part of the world, a tug at the string is a physical reminder that we can always come home. A gorgeous, tough, braided thread, shimmering in the sunlight through the canopies. The coil is beautiful. But it is also purposeful.

Every person's thread becomes tarnished, dishevelled in some way. No matter how strongly we want to anchor ourselves to ourselves, we are swung and swayed by the world in such ways that strands break, or become stained. Family trauma, illness, assault, accidents, pandemics... The potential ways each of our threads could be damaged are plentiful.

The thread is a timeline, a lifeline. Think of it as a visual, longitudinal take on micromorts[7]: each time the thread is damaged, it leaves a mark, and these marks cumulatively affect the nature of the coil. Like Casey Jenkins[8] knitting a singular 15-metre passage with woollen yarn inserted in their cunt, staining it with whatever their body chooses to expel each day: traces of menstrual blood, or discharge. Sometimes seemingly nothing at all. But their knitted artefact, in its completion, shows a much fuller picture; the delicate but often visceral changes as Casey spotted or menstruated, bloody secretions embedded into threads knitted into other, bloodless threads. Some sections show few signs of bodily fluids, while others show signs of heavy flow, of uterine lining, of the ambiguous change in the colour of twine caused by other emissions. So too is our thread, our coil, stained and altered by life as we wade through it. Like Jenkins' work, the staining is organic, dictated by the ebb and flow of life events. However, unlike Jenkins' work, the twine is not only stained but is also weakened, its integrity tested, and, at times, overthrown.

There may be times where you are so beaten down, so utterly desperate, that your connection to self is reduced to nearly nothing. You are in reaction, in survival mode, activated, full of cortisol [9]. The harder your experience in that moment, the more the thread becomes damaged and tarnished. The more it is damaged, the less likely you are to find your way home, or even retrace your most recent steps. And as my gorgeous Steven suggested, some people can never find their way home.

Catherine Malabou's [10] exploration of this sense of disconnection provides an insight into this phenomenon at its most extreme: people whose threads to self were cut so suddenly, intense, or cruelly, that a new persona is created which may have nothing to do with a person's prior sense of self. Like Athena being birthed from Zeus's head, those of us whose threads were truly cut may feel like they were born where they stood. They inhabit mature bodies without history, and unless this incision is somehow redressed, without a future.

For those whose exposure to trauma is momentary or singular, and who have the right privileges and opportunities, recovery can be very real and substantial. The thread can be re-anchored or re-tied to a nearby touchstone. The damage may be heavy, but it is reversible. This process is far more complex for queer, trans, and/or Jewish people. Our line connecting us to ourselves is sometimes worn down daily, hourly, whether by homophobia, transphobia, white supremacy, or capitalism. Our queer, gender-expansive, Jewish selves are ill-fitting within a straight, cisgender, white world, and the consequences of that mismatch are often severe.

Belonging to Ourselves

This book has explored belonging in a community sense, the rifts and connective tissue which connect us with our various communities and social groups. We have also discussed embodiment, where trauma can be felt and how it manifests physically. However, if we are to understand queer Jewish experiences (or any other experiences of inter-secting points of marginalization or difference which are beyond the scope of this book), we need to consider how it is that we belong to ourselves. This is the feeling that one's body, mind, and spirit are aligned and congruent; the sense that you belong in your body, and that your body belongs to you. Many of my interviewees, both in this study and in other queer and trans research projects [11, 12], dis-cussed the overwhelming sense of disconnec-tion they had felt from themselves. For some this was to do transness, with the so-called "misalignment"[13] between a person's under-standing of their gender and the way their

Jonathan: I kind of just stayed on the fringes in high school socially. I was mostly just friends with a bunch of geeky teen-age boys. I kind of knew that I wasn't really a lesbian. I knew that I was attracted to people of an array of different genders but I also knew that [...] even though I was attracted to boys I didn't want to be anyone's girl-friend. So I didn't really explore that. I did date a girl in high school. But I was really discon-nected from my body and it didn't really go well so it didn't really go anywhere.

body is constructed. For others, the disconnection was more behavioural, or mental; simply trying to put away thoughts or feelings around sexuality. Simi-larly, many of my interviewees also discussed an inner disconnection from Jew-ishness, with varying degrees of mourning or apathy towards this loss. These are all reactions to the world we live in, and the communities we try to engage with, but it is important to consider how internalized stigmas can change one's relationship to oneself first and foremost.

Internalized homo- and transphobia can wreak havoc on a person's well-being, fuelling risky sexual behaviours, substance use, and poor mental health [14–16]. Less is known about internalized antisemitism, arguably because we have come up with a euphemism which seems to have become almost cute and dated: a "self-hating Jew"[17]. Perhaps this is due to the fact that this term has been truly worn out by Jews across the political spectrum, as a means of denigrating other Jews who sit on either side of the fence on topics such as the Occupation [18, 19]. Nonetheless, existing as racialized "Others" within a country with a history such as Australia's can take its toll [20], even if we were accepted as post-World War II refugees [21, 22]. Anti-Semitic sentiments and sometimes-subtle processes of othering have always existed in Australia [23, 24] as they do globally, and continue to exist today [25, 26]. These messages penetrate the membrane separating our Selves from Everything Else and, even if they are largely rejected, leave traces behind.

These fragments of hatred remain as irritants, as foreign bodies for the Self to negotiate, to attempt to expel or dissolve. But every moment that we carry these fragments within us is a moment where we are forced to no longer feel entirely *within ourselves*. The discomfort, the pain, the disruption to our internal machinations, they all cause a rift that sets us at odds with ourselves. If we are lucky, we become conscious of these fragments, and actively work towards removing these negative outside influences from our selves. Whether it is racial justice, class consciousness, or the increasing mass of people diving into the true complexity of gender and sexuality, there have always been collectivized and internal processes of resistance to self-hatred at work [27]. But that is active work, and it can be "hard, heavy work" [28] too. And so these fragments of colonialism, white supremacy, and cisheteropatriarchy remain in our bodies and in our spirits, causing a division between us and ourselves through the cognitive dissonance of internalized racial, gender, and sexual stigma.

All of these considerations leave me with a set of questions: what does it mean to exist at an intersection of multiple points of forced separation from myself? Is there even an "authentic self" being held hostage here, or have its captors failed to mention its demise in the process of our negotiation? Are we working towards returning to some kind of innate purity, or towards an emergent bricolage of old and new, of scarred flesh neighbouring the smooth skin of new growth? In short, are our threads to our new selves recoverable and repairable?

It takes many hands and many ways to mend what society destroys, and that mending is not singular in its nature. Many of the people I had spoken to discussed reassembling threads, re-tying previously severed connections within themselves, and between themselves and others. Although this section is not exhaustive, it is intended to illustrate some approaches queer and trans Jews have towards reconnection and *rebraiding the thread*.

Several of my interviewees discussed a multiplicity of these connective threads,

> **Madelaine:** A lot of my friends have kids and they're raising them outside a religious environment which makes sense because most people aren't religious. [. . .] I wouldn't necessarily send my kids to a Jewish school but [. . .] I would have that weird default assumption of "that's how you raise a family" and "that's how you instill values". Even though I don't have that sense of [the] fire and brimstone part of the Old Testament.
>
> **Shosh:** Sure.
>
> **Madelaine:** I don't have that Leviticus guilt and yet I feel like that's a way that you frame your ethics and frame your view of the world. So it's not very logical, but again it's inextricably linked and I think that that's part of the Holocaust survivor part as well. [. . .] If there's that much suffering you have to hold a thread. And I feel bad that I don't have kids as part of that because that would be the next piece of legacy. Like I've let that bit down. [. . .] So you've got to keep the other connections going.

running almost the full gamut from the very inner to the global. They each expressed the difficulty of having to sit with the pressure of reproduction, of the commandment to raise a child not only healthily but also Jewishly, to provide a counterpoint to the destruction of our people. This is but one side of the intersections of pressure, one which is equally matched by the queer pressure to resist parenthood, to be what Lee Edelman[29] calls a true "synthomosexual" who is resistant to the very notion of reproduction, of the importance of the child as the carrier of history and cultural knowledge.

In a way, Edelman makes a good point. Queerness is not passed down from parent to child, no matter how ardently some biologists argue to the contrary[30]. Therefore, it is important to contemplate why it is that we obsess with lineages of birth, as opposed to lineages of discipline, of political activism, of cyclical elder-youth dynamics, of shared experiences, and of mutual aid and growth. While I think Edelman could do with a decent dose of a chemical relaxant of his choosing to counter that death drive-obsessive grouchiness, he highlights a very interesting point about the strength of queer traditions of cultural survival, as opposed to the heteronormative script about the supposedly unproblematic roles of both parent and child in the passing-on of knowledge. Like other cultures which have survived oppression and outright attempts at total excision, queers pass on our culture through songs, stories, sex, and art. Queer beats, clubs, and other spaces which are constantly forced to exist in the cracks between normative architecture (both physical and metaphysical) are vital spaces for knowledge transmission, for kin to connect with kin, whether for a night or a lifetime [31].

There are so many considerations when it comes to how both Jews and queers speak of our dis/connection from ourselves and others. We juggle responsibilities to our lineages and traditions alongside our own vision of our life trajectories. We do this while having to consider the ways we can and cannot realistically adhere to what is asked of us by our ancestors, for better or for worse. So do we finish Hitler's work of destroying the Jewish people by not having (Jewish) children[32], or do we finish the Mattachine Society's work of capitulating full-scale to cisheteronormative, capitalist, beige-themed family structures by having children [33, 34]? Either way, you are bound to feel shame, if not within then from outside yourself.

In order to make sense of this longitudinal perspective on belonging, both to ourselves and to others, we need to consider this notion of legacy. "Legacy" carries a different affect to "lineage"; a legacy is something bold, something earned, something quite possibly worth dying for. In our extended metaphor, lineage is the purpose of our coiled thread, but legacy is its beauty. Lineage in itself is not enough of a driver, because the task of truly envisioning the ways we are haunted by centuries of ancestors is nebulous and lifelong [35]. But legacy is immediate, it is something you can (often physically) point to, something you can anchor yourself to. Legacies of queerness and transness are brick and mortar venues where riots started, glory holes in university bathrooms and bikie bar toilets, the continuing existence of queer Houses, Families, activist groups, organizers (of both the political and party variety), and communes. Legacies of Jewishness are our food, our traditions, our bone-dry humour. Our collective legacies are our boldly told stories of survival in the face of overwhelming odds.

It always feels tenuous to try to find comparison points between different marginalized groups. Doing this kind of point-to-point comparison between different experiences of marginalization can run the risk of exaggerating similarities, erasing differences, or missing out on the nuances of one or both compared parties. This happens most often when a person with only the lived experience of one (or none) of the groups in question attempts to theorize crossovers without fully considering the inextricable differences that exist between both individuals and groups. However, in the case of this project, I and all my interviewees exist at precisely the kind of cross-marginalized nexus that provides us with unique insight. None of what I say, or have said so far, will resonate for every single queer or trans Jew. But as Janet Jakobsen suggests in the title of their essay: queers are like Jews, aren't they[36]?

Elsa: I now have some people who are really, really dear to me. I have a friend of mine who is like a friend, but also somewhat a life partner who is queer and Jewish. And doing Jewishness with them has been one of the most healing and validating experiences ever because you just feel held in these two parts of yourself that have never been held together in that way. And it doesn't even have to be purposeful because you just exist and you just are both those things. It's just a real synthesis. You know, it's smooth. It doesn't feel like a performance. It just is. I think that's been one of the most validating and healing things to get to share that, that joint space with another person who gets it and feels it and knows it in their body in a similar way.

So we find ourselves at a crossroads, between multiple beautiful legacies that are as much at loggerheads as they are dovetailing. To me, Jewishness and queerness/transness are like a bickering old couple: they are never going to truly separate because they are both intrinsically tied to each other in a variety of ways. Then, it is up to us to settle arguments and find common ground between them, for the sake of the proverbial couple's sanity, but more realistically for the sake of our own. There's only so long you can listen to someone kvetch about the dishes, or be witness to a person receiving the cold shoulder from their partner. We need to therefore ask ourselves: how do we get the Jewish Zayda and queer Bubbe inside us to get along?

It might seem like the origin point for this resolution is relational, whether in terms of the solidarity efforts and re-understandings of our complexities in geopolitical and anti-colonial terms. And yes, exposure to the experiences of others, particularly those who are (at least superficially) radically different from us, is a fantastic catalyst. However, the lessons embedded within these encounters quickly ameliorate if our internal world is not attuned to its own state. If our self-understanding is only defined by proxy, by deference to liturgy or vague liberal guidelines or other points external to ourselves, we risk atrophying our strongest bond – the bond between us and ourselves. Throughout my interviews, there is a sense of connection to self returned time and time again as a protective factor, as a mediator between what the outside world feeds us and what we are capable of incubating within ourselves. After all, if we were to simply ingest external values and narratives whole, making our stomachs into nothing more than holding places for these feelings and ideas, we would soon rupture. If there's something Jews in particular know how to do well, then, it is to digest copious quantities of whatever is coming our way[1].

This is where belonging to ourselves, an active and continuous process of self-attunement, becomes most valuable. This process is more often visible in its absence than in its presence. Take, for example, the hushed tones which accompany any conversation about Israel amongst Jews; it is a subject so taboo that even I feared addressing it in the pages of this book. The Australian Jewry has arrived at the point that it is in its relationship to the Israeli apartheid state through strict discompassion and non-discussion, deferring to the positions of greater (colonial) powers [37], and supplanting our basic empathetic response in favour of a narrative of collective (Jewish) survival. How else can you explain the persistent response of "we do what we have to in order to survive" amongst many Australian Jews in the face of the horrors Palestinians endure under Israeli rule? With the exception of those who are truly numbed to the world, whether by trauma or some kind of sociopathy, it is impossible to not have an intense response to the footage of dead children, bombed cemeteries, and crowded encampments which depict the daily life for the majority of Palestinians living in occupied Palestine.

---

1 Kreplach, kugel, matzah balls, etc.

Yet, dominant narratives prevail. These narratives sit in our guts like stones, undigested and therefore barred from either passing through our bodies or being otherwise cleanly excised. I know that I have felt this weight, trying to understand why it is that my childhood fear of violence felt tempered with other sensations. I grew up afraid, but when I was told that it was Palestinians I had to fear, I could not find it in myself to agree. I remember distinctly being at school on the commemoration day of the Nakba, otherwise known as the beginning of the Occupation. During lunch, several Palestinian children ran up to me from outside the school gate and pelted rocks towards me and the other children. When I spoke to my mother about this incident later that day, she explained that they were retaliating but did not explain what it was they were retaliating against. I did not understand what made me deserve a stone to my face. But I also understood that to feel compelled to throw a stone in another's face, one had to have a very good reason.

This was the contradiction I lived with for many years, and it was not until I had begun connecting further with both others and myself that I understood this scenario to its full extent. In connecting with others, including both Palestinians and other Indigenous peoples who were at war with a colonizing force, I understood the political background for experiences such as my younger self's. But in connecting with myself, I understood more deeply the fire that burnt in the guts of those children, and the fire that burnt within myself. I also came to understand how I too had been throwing stones, in my own way. I would be a hypocrite if I were to say that I would resort to non-violence if put in the same position. In fact, non-violence has facilitated nothing but further victimization in my own life. Whether that non-violence manifested as being agreeable in intimate and partner violence scenarios (which I have a lifetime of experience with) or refusing to protect myself when my personhood was being violated (e.g. being subjected to unnecessary genital examinations as part of transitioning), passivity rarely earned me anything more than scars and shame.

We often resort to discussions of psychology when looking at both Jewish and queer experiences, but this psychological lens does not always interconnect with greater systemic issues at play. Concepts such as "minority stress" provide an incomplete overview of why a person or group may have negative life experiences and by extension experience negative psychological symptoms [38]. This is where taking a "reparative reading" [39] becomes "risky" in evaluating both Jewish and queer lived experience; there are taboos in both groups, and in their interweaving narratives, which do not provide a clean-cut perspective on the disruptive factors which affect the wellbeing of these groups.

In the case of queers, the dominant narrative of heteronormativity and cissexism is one of external subjugation, oppression, and persecution within a system hellbent on destroying us. And while this is true, we cannot fully comprehend queer life and its complexities without addressing issues such as lateral violence, class, and racial divides within communities, and the fact that many queers have access to mechanisms of oppression which are not unlike the ones that we portray as solely external forces. The queer landlord, debt collector, or serial abuser are not anomalies within an otherwise purely subjugated group of people; they are part of the tapestry of queer communities, and often leverage their queerness in order to further insert themselves and their exploitative tactics into the lives of others in their communities.

Jewish communities are no different. It is undeniable that we are subjected to antisemitism, and in some contexts Jewish persecution is truly alive and well [40]. However, our sense of persecution is not entirely explained by these factors alone. The reality is that much of contemporary Jewish suffering is ideological, caused by a strain of faux-survivalist racism furthered by Jews in power who are aligned with fascist ideals of purity and racial survival, such as former Israeli Prime Minister Benjamin Netanyahu [41]. The call is indeed coming from inside the house. Of course we have remained afraid for our lives long after the Shoah, but our fear has metastasized to such an extent that many of us have become aggressors rather than simply survivors. Only through introspection, through investigating the roots of our fears, can we understand how we have arrived at our current collective positions.

In avoiding the reality of how notions of collective purity and innocence have warped our personal perspectives, we have facilitated a process of self-abandonment which is now perpetuated interpersonally, intergenerationally, and internationally. Returning to a point made earlier in this chapter, we can see how existing in the liminal spaces between seemingly concrete definitions of our lives can illicit significant negative affects. If we choose to be neither "breeders" nor child-hating queers, we fail to belong; a real queer shame. If we choose to neither abandon Jewishness nor absolve our communities of the injustices they perpetuate in our collective name, we fail to belong – another source of shande. The mere admission that queers or Jews are flawed human beings capable of harm, both personal and systemic, forms such a strong taboo that it muddies our capacity to act out of compassion, reflexivity, and recognition of contextual complexity. When we think the fire burning inside us either belongs to us alone[2]

---

2 Whoever this "us" may be, e.g. queers, Jews, crips, fat people, etc.

or is something that should not exist within anyone at all, we inevitably neglect recognizing why fires may burn within others.

I hope that you, dear reader, are not mistaking my argument for personal exploration and introspection with any neoliberal notions of individualism. Our struggles, and the lessons learned from them, are perpetually interconnected. However, there are mechanisms within the human psyche which can either be harnessed to benefit collective harmony or to cause further insularity, and those mechanisms cannot be ignored when considering the complexities of lives such as those of queer Jews. Think of the thread discussed at the beginning of this chapter; it may have become withered and worn by time and other factors external to us. But its condition cannot be entirely dependent on the decisions of the three Fates [42]; our lives may be constricted by our circumstances, but our movements within them are still subject to the microcosm of daily and momentary actions we choose to take. When we allow our core human reactions to be supplanted by broader ideological frameworks, we risk not only disconnection from ourselves but also disconnection from others. Engaging with this process is not simple by any means. Ironically, it requires faith in the most basic way: faith that we are all working towards a shared humanity. This faith requires a certain level of disidentification [43], of holding what is dear to us close, but not so close that we entirely meld into it and leave the broader world behind. Insularity is a short-term healing salve at best, and a slowly-poisoning balm at worst.

Belonging to the World

It's easy to see how the histories of both queers and Jews have led to our contemporary approaches to collective safety. I have discussed these at length in previous chapters: both groups have endured centuries of oppression due to certain elements which, at least at a glance, cluster these peoples together. Whether we discuss shtetls or queer communes, there are valid reasons for both queers and Jews to hide away from the world which has often been so cold to us. But in the modern world, the majority of us are no longer relegated to ghettos, confined to segregated communities and secretive, illicit places of gathering. We exist in globalized societies, where we share neighbourhoods, streets, workplaces, and other public settings with people from a broad spectrum of experiences. Like us, many of these people belong to groups which have also relied (and in many cases still rely) on self-siloing as a means of survival. But it is rare to come across spaces, particularly public spaces, where any type of categorical segregation has produced positive outcomes for that space and the places it neighbours. When I think of modern-day insularity, I envision all-white gated communities and "respectable" public places rife with anti-homeless defensive architecture [44]. This is insularity based on keeping undesirables from entering, rather than maintaining its inhabitants safe from any legitimate outside threats.

In this sense, when we accept the process of self-belonging, we can also understand these delineated hegemonic spaces for what they are: a refusal to sit with the complexity of the world and our position within it. This refusal inevitably leads to disquietude within the spaces, as well as outside it (for those who have been denied entry). This is where heavily policed queer and Jewish spaces are arguably at their most violent and least productive. Recently, I took my partner to her very first experience of a synagogue service. At the heavily guarded gate, we were subjected to several minutes of questioning from one of the security officers: "Have you been here before?" "Do you know anyone who goes here?" "Why are you coming to this service?" I anticipated this process to some extent, having been a first-timer at a synagogue many times over my life as a semi-nomadic person. But to my partner, a non-Jew who was nonetheless interested and invested in Jewish experiences, this was truly shocking.

Jamaica: I think I operate a lot better in queer spaces. But I always combat the risks and the [. . .] questions and doubts that a hyper femme cis woman gets in those queer spaces. With the queer spaces mostly that I've encountered tended to be quite patriarchal. And even in those spaces my legitimacy was questioned.

Following the service, we discussed at length the purpose of this questioning process, which carried over from the synagogue gate and into the service itself, where our presence was questioned by multiple synagogue staff. Meanwhile, as my partner and I sat through the discomfort of having our very presence at the service questioned, a representative from an Israeli organization was invited to the pulpit to discuss the weekly Torah portion, using the opportunity to inject her speech with discussions of the necessity of the state of Israel to the Jewish people. The crowd hummed agreeably with her talk, which effortlessly glided over subjects such as Israel's corrupt government, their anti-Palestinian regime, and the poor living conditions of both Palestinians and "lesser" Israeli citizens. After all, Israel is ultimately the place where all Jews belong, and we as attendees living in Galut (exile) were privileged to have a person from our supposed homeland in attendance. Or so we were told.

There was no place for dialogue within this service, as there rarely is in these kinds of contemporary spaces. They enact a strict political delineation, a melding of Jewish culture and faith with viewpoints which are controversial at best and downright harmful at worst. As my partner and I debriefed after the service, I had to inform her that this was the status quo of Jewish institutions in Australia, and arguably across all diasporic Jewish communities. The powerlessness I felt, not even as a Palestinian but simply as an ally to Indigenous peoples the world over, reflected this process of quelling one's internal fire that I discussed in the previous section. This is certainly the case in academia, where anti-Zionist writers find themselves facing censure or expulsion due to their views on Israel-Palestine [45]. Matt [46] has even suggested that many queer Jews feel the need to "come out" (or not) about their anti-Zionist views due to the overwhelming pressure to conform to Zionist ideas about Israel, Palestine, and the Palestinian people. I was visibly outnumbered at this pro-Zionist synagogue service, and my partner was already so jolted by our cold and suspicious experiences of questioning that to speak up would have caused more turmoil than resolution. The shame within both of us, both in how we were treated and our silence in the face of such a rigid and violent political diatribe, was palpable.

I have had similar experiences traversing queer spaces. Often I am one of a small handful of trans women present, and most certainly within a minority of non-white people in attendance. And yet, much like going to this synagogue despite my knowledge of how the proceedings will go, I still find myself attending these queer spaces. Are these acts of defiance? Yes. But they are not simply attempts at expanding the political lenses of others in attendance, or shining a light, however small, in places that otherwise feel dark and hostile to people with my lived experience and perspectives. My presence in these spaces is a representation of the permeability that all insular spaces have the potential to internalize into their existence. This is because I do not belong in a synagogue in the same way that I do not belong in a queer party. First and foremost *I belong to myself, and I belong to the world.*

We can become bogged down in our discussions of how this or that institution, establishment, party, or other third space is exclusionary. Many times it is vital to challenge this exclusion, to attempt to improve the conditions of a particular space or place. I am no stranger to this: I spend much of my time outside of my studies working to improve conditions for queer and trans people in a variety of places. However, our focus on the exclusivity or inclusivity of any particular group or space can have a kind of gravitational effect. We can find ourselves immersed in processes of challenging and questioning to such an extent that we connect our identities and personal lives with these efforts. I can attest that my darkest moments of feeling isolated, excluded, and place-less have been at times where my energy was focused intensively on address-ing injustices in specific contexts (e.g. healthcare settings, queer social circles, Jewish institutions). It often feels like we are fighting within our own homes, which makes our departure or detachment from those places feel like the kind of landlessness I discussed in an earlier chapter; it can leave one desperate, conflicted, and often lead to either an abandonment of those spaces you are fighting within or an abandonment of oneself in order to continue to experi-ence some semblance of belonging within those spaces.

This is where the liminality of true belongingness can feel the most dis-cordant, abrasive, and uncomfortable. If our metric of belongingness lies with our ability to comfortably remain within strict and predetermined social, polit-ical, or geographic boundaries, then we are bound to either feel perpetually displaced or in a state of self-neglect. This is the irony of existing in societies where our lives are perpetually intertwined with thousands if not millions of others; belonging can no longer be reduced to physical places or ready-at-hand groups, and no group of people can entirely avoid contact with others [47]. Belonging, then, has become a bricolage, a matter of interpersonal and collec-tive alignment that cannot be reduced down to any singular identity or lived experience[3]. Where would my life be without the input of others who are dif-ferent to me? Where would theirs be without mine? We need to consider how we have shaped our mutual reality, and how can we continue to do so in ways that uphold the needs of those who are most vulnerable.

This idea of bricolage belongingness, of understanding oneself beyond the constraints of pre-existing social and cultural narratives, is at its most liber-atory. Through this lens, discomfort is an expected element, rather than a nuisance to be eliminated or avoided at all costs. How can anyone exist with-out discomfort? Even the most elite and self-segregated among us inevitably encounter people who challenge their ways of existing, and the impacts their lives have on the lives of others. When I say I belong to the world, I mean it in the most fundamental way. I breathe this air, I live on certain lands of cer-tain peoples, I am in contact with others who are both incredibly similar and radically different to myself on a daily basis. I belong here[4], whether I like it

3 This is a distinction from how bricolage has been used to uphold Settler-Colonialism through the selective appropriation of Indigeneity into a greater colonial narrative [48].
4 At least until space colonies become a reality.

or not. Belonging is an active, relational, and internal process which we must constantly attend to. This active process of sensing and connecting with one's belongingness can be spiritual [49], cultural [50], or even political [51], but it is never a feeling that can be achieved passively. I belong to the world because I have a duty to it, and it has a duty to me. The matters which define this duty vary from person to person, from place to place. But they are ultimately part and parcel of belonging to this world. Any other experience of inclusion or exclusion, of myself or others, is contained within this broader experience of belonging.

Throughout my interviews there was a common thread around notions of belonging. No matter how attached my interviewees were to a particular identity or signifier of that identity (e.g. a synagogue or a biological family), the places where they experienced true belonging were most commonly defined by the relationships and affective atmospheres particular people or spaces facilitated within them. That is to say, there is a significant difference between being a member of a particular group or place and feeling like one legitimately *belonged* there. Membership can conjure up a variety of ligatures: you must pay a fee, you must abide by certain codes, you carry a card (or other signifier) which denotes your membership and often excludes you from being a member elsewhere. Belonging, in its truest sense, is much more fluid and responsive: you belong somewhere not only because you have fulfilled your duties but because your needs have also been fulfilled. This is where many of my interviewees expressed feeling a disconnection from Jewishness in particular: the price of being a member of a particular congregation or community was too high compared to the potential benefits of having a membership. Often the "price" was exposure to homophobia, transphobia, racism, ableism, and restrictive values around what relationships, friendships, or a successful life had to look like.

When we shift our perspective away from these specific groups or circles and towards our vision of our relationship with humanity more broadly, we can gain a different understanding of how belonging can be felt and understood. Membership is static – belongingness is an action. Membership is renewed rigidly and bureaucratically – belongingness is renewed through relationality. Membership is intellectual and ideological – belongingness is felt in the body, in the moment, and often beyond the moment. In order to understand queer Jewish belonging, we therefore need to think beyond clubs, institutions, cliques, and so on. We need to consider who aligns themself with us, and who we align ourselves with. We need to consider what lies at the core of this alignment, and which aspect of our being is being serviced by this alignment. Queer Jewish belonging must be understood as part of a broader network of belonging, one which all peoples are given the opportunity to belong to daily. Our individual threads, those ever-diminishing strings which connect us to our histories and our cores, cannot be strengthened alone: they must be braided into those of others. We are tethered to the world, as it is tethered to us.

References

[1] Benjamin AE. *Present Hope: Philosophy, Architecture, Judaism.* Psychology Press, 1997.

[2] Pearl MB. *AIDS Literature and Gay Identity: The Literature of Loss.* Routledge, 2013.

[3] LaCapra D. *Writing History, Writing Trauma.* JHU Press, 2014.

[4] Hirsch M. *The Generation of Postmemory: Writing and Visual Culture after the Holocaust.* Columbia University Press, 2012.

[5] Bauer H. Burning sexual subjects: Books, homophobia and the Nazi destruction of the Institute of Sexual Science in Berlin. In: Partington G, Smyth A (eds). *Book Destruction from the Medieval to the Contemporary.* London: Palgrave Macmillan UK, pp. 17–33.

[6] Vonnegut K. Slaughterhouse-Five. 1969. *N Y Laurel.*

[7] Ahmad N, Peterson N, Torella F. The Micromort: A unit for comparing and communicating risk to patients. *Int J Clin Pract* 2015; 69: 515–517.

[8] Jenkins C. Casting off my womb: 28 day durational performance artwork. *Casey Jenkins,* <https://casey-jenkins.com/works/casting-off-my-womb/> (2013, accessed 8 June 2020).

[9] Staufenbiel SM, Penninx BWJH, Spijker AT, et al. Hair cortisol, stress exposure, and mental health in humans: A systematic review. *Psychoneuroendocrinology* 2013; 38: 1220–1235.

[10] Malabou C. *The Ontology of the Accident: An Essay on Destructive Plasticity.* Wiley, 2012.

[11] Rosenberg S. Coming in: Queer narratives of sexual self-discovery. *J Homosex* 2018; 65: 1788–1816.

[12] Rosenberg S, Tilley PJM, Morgan J. "I Couldn't Imagine My Life Without It": Australian trans women's experiences of sexuality, intimacy, and gender-affirming hormone therapy. *Sex Cult* 2019; 23: 962–977.

[13] Imborek KL, Graf EM, McCune K. Preventive health for transgender men and women. *Semin Reprod Med* 2017; 35: 426–433.

[14] Ross MW, Berg RC, Schmidt AJ, et al. Internalised homonegativity predicts HIV-associated risk behavior in European men who have sex with men in a 38-country cross-sectional study: Some public health implications of homophobia. *BMJ Open* 2013; 3: e001928.

[15] Chard AN, Finneran C, Sullivan PS, et al. Experiences of homophobia among gay and bisexual men: Results from a cross-sectional study in seven countries. *Cult Health Sex* 2015; 17: 1174–1189.

[16] Morandini JS, Blaszczynski A, Dar-Nimrod I, et al. Minority stress and community connectedness among gay, lesbian and bisexual Australians: A comparison of rural and metropolitan localities. *Aust N Z J Public Health* 2015; 39: 260–266.

[17] Jaspal R. *Antisemitism and Anti-Zionism: Representation, Cognition and Everyday Talk.* Routledge, 2016.

[18] Friedman M. Jewish self-hatred, moral criticism, and autonomy. *Pers Auton Soc Oppression Philos Perspect* 2015; 203–222.

[19] Cohen S. *That's Funny You Don't look Antisemitic.* Shepheard Walwyn Publishers, 2019.

[20] Seet AZ. Serving the white nation: Bringing internalised racism within a sociological understanding. *J Sociol* 2019; 1440783319882087.

[21] Jayasuriya L. *Transforming a "White Australia": Issues of Racism and Immigration.* SSS Publications, 2012.

[22] Muller DC. Doomed from the start: Australia's rejection of Dr IN Steinberg's Kimberley Plan. *Aust J Jew Stud*; 32.

[23] Turnbull MJ. *Safe Haven: Records of the Jewish Experience in Australia.* National Archives of Australia, 1999.

[24] Medding P. *From Assimilation to Group Survival: A Political and Sociological Study of an Australian Jewish Community.* Cheshire, 1968.

[25] Jones J. Confronting Reality: Anti-Semitism in Australia Today. *Jew Polit Stud Rev* 2004; 16: 89–103.

[26] Nathan J. *Report on Antisemitism in Australia 2019.* NSW: The Executive Council of Australian Jewry, 2019.

[27] Yu N. Consciousness-Raising and Critical Practice. In: Consciousness-Raising. Routledge, 2018, pp. 1–13.

[28] Freire P. *Pedagogy of Hope: Reliving Pedagogy of the Oppressed.* A&C Black, 2014.

[29] Edelman L. *No Future: Queer Theory and the Death Drive.* Duke University Press, 2004.

[30] Balthazart J. *The Biology of Homosexuality.* Oxford University Press, USA, 2012.

[31] Muñoz JE, Chambers-Letson J, Nyong'o T, et al. *Cruising Utopia, 10th Anniversary Edition: The Then and There of Queer Futurity.* NYU Press, 2019.

[32] Glaser G. *Strangers to the Tribe: Portraits of Interfaith Marriage.* Houghton Mifflin, 1997.

[33] Cimino KW. *Gay Conservatives: Group Consciousness and Assimilation.* Routledge, 2012.

[34] Velte KC. From the Mattachine Society to Megan Rapinoe: Tracing and telegraphing the conformist/visionary divide in the LGBT-Rights Movement. *Univ Richmond Law Rev* 2019; 54: 799.

[35] Brager S. J. *Doykeit: We Will Outlive Them.* Solomon J Brager, 2018.

[36] Jakobsen JR. Queers are like Jews, aren't they? Analogy and alliance politics. *Queer Theory Jew Quest* 2003; 64–89.

[37] Burchill S. Israel-Palestine: Part two—Australian foreign policy and the Israel-Palestine conflict—avoiding the colonialist narrative. In: Burchill S (ed). *Misunderstanding International Relations: A Focus on Liberal Democracies.* Singapore: Springer, pp. 63–83.

[38] Riggs DW, Treharne GJ. Decompensation: A novel approach to accounting for stress arising from the effects of ideology and social norms. *J Homosex* 2017; 64: 592–605.

[39] Sedgwick EK. *Touching Feeling.* Duke University Press, 2003.

[40] Taguieff P-A. *Rising from the Muck: The New Anti-Semitism in Europe.* Ivan R. Dee, 2004.

[41] Keren M. Benjamin Netanyahu and Online Campaigning in Israel's 2019 and 2020 Elections.

[42] Holzman RS. The legacy of Atropos, the fate who cut the thread of life. *Anesthesiology* 1998; 89: 241–249.

[43] Muñoz JE. *Disidentifications: Queers of Color and the Performance of Politics.* U of Minnesota Press, 2013.

[44] Smith N, Walters P. Desire lines and defensive architecture in modern urban environments. *Urban Stud* 2018; 55: 2980–2995.

[45] Robinson WI, Griffin MS. *We Will Not Be Silenced: The Academic Repression of Israel's Critics.* AK Press, 2017.

[46] Matt LE. Queer, Anti-Zionist, & Jewish: Reimagining Jewish Identity through Queer Politics.

[47] Ahmadi N. Globalisation, postmodernity and migration–Rethinking cultural identity. In: Launikari, M., & Puukari, S. (eds) *Multicultural Guidance and Counselling: Theoretical Foundations and Best Practices in Europe*, CIMO 2005, 99.

[48] Barker AJ. *(Re-) Ordering the New World: Settler Colonialism*, Space, and Identity. 2013 [Doctoral thesis, university of Leicester].

[49] Chin SS. I am a human being, and I belong to the world: Narrating the intersection of spirituality and social identity. *J Transform Educ* 2006; 4: 27–42.

[50] Tokunaga T, Tokunaga T, Liu. *Learning to Belong in the World.* Springer, 2018.

[51] Schulze-Engler F. Once were internationalists? Postcolonialism, disenchanted solidarity and the right to belong in a world of globalized modernity. In: *Reworking Postcolonialism.* Springer, 2015, pp. 19–35.

· 7 ·

AN UN-CONCLUSION

Like a good Jewish princess I intended to write a nice, formal concluding chapter which brings together all the concepts and experiences discussed throughout this book. It was going to be very professional and prove that under all the jokes, pop culture debris, and emotional diatribes lies a stone-cold academic professional. Instead, I find myself compelled to write a different kind of chapter. First, allow me one last autoethnographic frivolity – a slice of life as these words are being typed. I have spent the past several weeks living in spare rooms of some of my beloveds, having become too physically unwell to remain living in my upstairs apartment. My pain has been oscillating on a scale between "barely bearable" and "one of the more sexually divisive scenes from the Hellraiser franchise". I am surrounded by friends and lovers who have been carrying me through this elongated inner uprising of my yet-to-be-fully-diagnosed illness, and their attempts to provide care and doting have been met with the kind of resistance normally reserved for a veterinarian visit. I have been a feral cat hissing at the back of the cage, clawing and spitting because anything else feels intrinsically against my nature. I am grateful for those who have withstood my pitiful lashes as they coaxed me into their arms. Their softness from without has created a softness within, and their nourishment forms a bedrock to this final chapter.

The Escalation

I began writing this chapter on October 21, 2023. On October 7, 2023, following a Palestinian Resistance attack on settlers near the Gaza strip[1], Israel formally declared war on Palestine and began bombing the Gaza Strip. As I write, I realize that by the time these words meet the gaze of a stranger, we may be living in a radically different political landscape. But all I can do is document this moment, and pray it meets my future self and my future readers in a better, rather than worse, world. A mere two weeks into this escalation, the death toll caused by Israeli airstrikes in Palestine is in the thousands. Every person in my life with even a marginal proximity to Palestine is horrified, and protests have been happening every few days across the country. The propaganda has been immediate and striking, both from within and outside of the Jewish community. I am finding myself witnessing something both terrifyingly new and numbingly familiar. I am falling asleep to Al Jazeera, to the sound of missiles annihilating civilians and crushing vital architecture both contemporary and ancient. In doing so I find myself enacting a type of twisted solidarity ritual with those who fall asleep to these same sounds and never wake again.

This escalating genocide has unveiled many truths to the world which so many of us have carried within us for so long. We are now seeing a global revelation around the true cruelty of Zionism, the fascist machinations which created the nation-state of Israel, and how versatile colonizing forces have become at shaping and moulding Jews to do their dirty work. In many ways this is one of the most terrifying political consequences of the creation of Israel via Palestinian genocide: this is just another stage in the scapegoating of Jews to fit the nationalistic and militaristic tactics of European and American colonization. The *Muscular Jew* would like the events of the past eight decades to be remembered as a linear growth in the nature of the Jewish people, evolving from the wretches of an entire continent to a righteous group protecting their biblically affirmed land by any means necessary. The *Muscular Jew* wants you to think that all Jews fight for is justified by our history, by our own genocide – a cosmic jiu jitsu match where we have at last gotten out of a centuries-long headlock and proceeded to triumph. But we all know better now, and many of us always have.

I am not using this closing chapter as a soapbox, not in an egotistical way at least. This book explores the vitality and complexity of queerness within

---

1 Which was initially attributed to Hamas only to later be withdrawn.

Judaism, and specifically within Jewish communities in so-called Australia. Across these chapters, I could not help but include the ways in which queer Jewishness inevitably must confront its relationship to Zionism, the Israeli regime, and the concept of a Jewish ethnostate. In every single interview I conducted, every conversation about my thesis, or any time I have discussed queer Jewishness at any length, I have found thoughts of the Israeli regime echoing through my mind. The Israeli regime is in many ways a unique geopolitical propaganda machine which has katamari'd queerness into its national chauvinism with great care. "Pinkwashing" in the context of the Israeli regime has been a growing concern in liberatory politics and resistance to the occupation; however, the issue is not simply a matter of softening Israel's image via projections of queer acceptance but also creating a binary between supposedly homo-loving Israelis and homophobic Palestinians [1]. I won't insult the intellect of the reader by addressing this binary in any real depth: if you have read this far then you know that arbitrary dichotomies of this scale are *always* created to distract from the paradoxes, falsehoods, and complexities which underly them. When a violent nation-state tells me it wants a queer Jewish cripple like myself among its ranks, it is my duty to think critically and understand whose lives I will inevitably destroy if I were to accept this Devil's Deal. Then, it is my duty to spit in that nation's face.

The Hand That Feeds

I began this book talking about my fear of biting the hand that feeds, particularly in the context of academia. Since writing those words several years ago, I have increasingly thought not so much about the hand as I have about what it has been feeding me. As a Jew born in so-called Israel, am I biting the hand that feeds by criticizing Israel? As a Jew living in so-called Australia, am I biting the hand that feeds by criticizing Australia? As a queer Jew, am I biting the hand that feeds by criticizing "LGBT-inclusive" Jewish spaces who refuse to acknowledge the Palestinian genocide? I have been told time and again to be grateful for the existence of each of these entities: grateful for the supposed safety Israel provides me as a Jew, for the Australian nation which allowed me to permanently enter its borders and access its (slightly higher) quality of life, for the Jewish spaces which have decided queers can come through their doors if they wish. I do not find safety in a Jewish state as a Jew in the same way that I do not find safety in an Australian nation as an Australian citizen: these governments systematically devalue their own citizens and maintain caste and class systems which pit the populace against itself. I am too crippled, too queer, too "unemployable", too fat, and frankly *too Jewish* to ever thrive in either of these colonies. I also do not find comfort in supposedly queer-friendly synagogues and services which carry on about Jewish oppression and refuse to recognize the table-turning reality of a genocide being enacted in our name. Tasting their blood in my mouth, a fresh bitemark in their proverbial hand, I can tell you now that I no longer wish to be fed this way.

I find myself fantasizing with my Palestinian friend Lyla about retiring to Falastin together. We tell each other that this time the world might actually do something to end the occupation. We both believe it. It almost feels like confessing a deep fantasy or talking about a celebrity crush. It's a complex series of actions away, but those actions seem feasible, swimming in a lake of hope. I tell them "I'll make the pitas", knowing they've got the knafeh covered. I find myself thinking: *this* is the hand I'd like to feed from. The hands of my friends, the hands of those working with me towards liberation of all oppressed peoples, the hands of my loves and strangers who are so free from suffering that they have enough to spare for a passer-by. I want to *be* a hand that feeds.

Resisting Resistance

If we're going to talk about liberatory resistance, we also need to talk about its shadow side, of excessive or ill-directed resistance. At the beginning of this chapter I reflected on my recent experience as a hand-biter extraordinaire. This visceral aversion to care is not some free-floating personality trait – it is a core aspect of myself that has been hammered in by my lived experience. I am prone to biting hands because time and time again they have served me poison. A lifetime of hope distorting into something ghoulish: nations meant to protect me turning out to be my biggest source of violence and abuse; communities meant to reflect and galvanize my queerness and Jewishness transforming into social chasms and dead ends; relationships meant to be built on mutuality and commonality winding up reflecting the very same social hierarchies I hoped we were opposing together. It is very easy to develop a protective coating so effective that it not only (supposedly) prevents harm but actively hurts those attempting to move past it.

If there is one thing I have learned during my time writing this book it's that resistance must be utilized correctly. I completed this book in the face of a pandemic, severe chronic illness, financial precarity, secondary houselessness, multiple experiences of intimate abuse, and the renewed eruption of a devastating genocide in my birthplace and in my people's name. I could not have made it through even one of these confronting life experiences if I did not allow care to come through, if I did not *resist my resistance*. If it weren't for the queers, Jews, transsexuals, and other radical freaks in my life, I would not be writing these words. If I did not have folks in my life who could discern between meaningful and trauma-driven resistance, between justified refusal and reactive self-defence, I could never have come this far. In the same way that it is my duty to resist oppression, violence, and propaganda; it is also my duty to accept love, care, and compassion.

Most importantly, I have come to recognize that resistance which is borne out of a fear of indignity, broken trust, or harm is resistive energy that can be transformed into something more liberatory. The media is currently flooded with Zionist Jews living in diaspora bemoaning their fear of retribution due to some vague spectre of rising antisemitism in the wake of increased anti-Zionism. The mental conquest of their Zionist upbringing is so complete that they cannot see the macroscopic mechanisms that have led to this fear. The conflation of Jewishness with Zionism, of Jews with the state of Israel, and of Jewish religious practices with rampant nationalism has made these people feel isolated. This is despite the fact that these complaints come from people at the very epicentre of Jewish life in diaspora: they are Rabbis and Cantors and syn-agogue philanthropists and long-term residents of the various Jewish enclaves spread across Australia, or descendants of these well-established community leaders and members. They are the people who are not troubled or repulsed by seeing an armed guard standing between them and their place of worship. They are the people who have stamped out any opposition to Zionist dialogue within the vast majority of their social and professional networks either by chronic avoidance or sheer hostility. They are the "queer-friendly" folks who refuse to see how their implicit attitudes and microaggressions marginalize and edge out non-normative peoples, and by extension the radical politics many of those peoples practice.

Now, with all the guns, national-power-by-proxy, and community and faith practices which have been fine-tuned to eliminate words like "Palestine" and "occupation" from their life, Jewish Zionists in the diaspora *still* picture themselves as victims. They cannot envision a less lonely world because they have bought the lie that this is un-lonely as it gets. The tragic reality is that by conceiving contemporary Jewish life through this lens, Zionists allow *per-ceived* threats to their safety and wellbeing to distract them from the *very real* threats facing all of us tangled in the web of the Israeli occupation. It can be terrifying to stare Zionist violence in the face, to see how many relationships and communities in the Jewish diaspora hinge on a tacit acceptance of Palestinian deaths, and to acknowledge that Jewish peoples' suffering is only as meaningful and unique as our response to it. It is hard to let go of a historical narrative which places us at the bottom of every ladder, justifies Jewish survival by any means, and perpetuates *Muscular Judaism* as the only prophylactic to a second Shoah.

These experiences are spiritually challenging, relationally challenging, and certainly communally challenging, especially with the ever-looming threat of ostracization for Jews who dare speak out against Israeli oppression. However, all those fears and concerns are not a wall to hit but a veil to push through. Past the threshold, behind the curtain of "benevolent" Zionism and Pollyanna "queer acceptance" and tepid Acknowledgements of Country[2] on stolen land lies a flourishing world of connection and beauty. For every pro-Israel person I have lost due to my politics, I have gained handfuls of comrades from all over the world. Every hostile conversation about the Israeli occupation that I have is countered by many conversations where we dream about a future where we are all free. For every instance where someone attempts to subvert my queerness and Jewishness into anti-Arab or anti-Muslim sentiment, I find moments of comfort with the many queers, Jews, Arabs, and Muslims in my life who all know that we can and do coexist in harmony. Not to date myself or minimize the meaningfulness and challenges of pushing past these deeply entrenched concerns, but I have implored and will continue to implore anyone faced with these dilemmas to "feel the fear and do it anyway"[2], as it were. And if you are reading this and want to take the leap, I will tell you this: we will be there to catch you.

Not in Our Name

The chasm between the Jewish narrative of survival against adversity and the reality of Jewish life in the diaspora, with its many privileges and its collective weaponization in modern-day colonial efforts, is one that is becoming increasingly difficult to reconcile. You will have found yours truly grappling with this rift of cognitive dissonance throughout this book. This book was intended to highlight queer Jewish complexity, diversity, and most importantly vitality. Inevitably, that has included discussions of queer Jewish marginalization in the

---

2 Made further tepid by a total absence of Aboriginals in attendance.

Australian colony, especially layered experiences ranging from discomfort to outright rejection within multiple identity-based communities. But I fear I may have still failed in my mission to fully express queer Jewish "Australians" ' relationship to violence. It is difficult to discuss queer Jewish experiences in Australia, or any nation-state, without fully acknowledging the violence inherent in the existence of that nation-state. Yes, I have discussed the systemic violence of oppressive Australian governmental policies such as the White Australia Policy, and the direct violence experienced by queer Jewish people who have been targeted for their gender, sexuality, race, or religious background (perceived or otherwise). But I have neglected to touch on the unique violence that queer Jews in the Australian diaspora are *invited to enact*.

One of the biggest protest slogans to have emerged in response to the recent escalation in the Palestinian genocide has been "Not In Our Name", popularized by Jewish Voice for Peace and If Not Now, two United States–based Jewish protest collectives [3]. These four words reveal an aspect of diasporic Jewish life that many of us have had to face: that the narrative justifying this genocide is based on a core belief that every single killing is being done in the name of all Jews. While saying that the killing of Palestinians is not being done in our name[3] shows solidarity, we also need to confront the other ways in which we might implicitly sign our names to this genocide. When I say queer Jews living in Australia are invited to enact violence, I am not just talking about the ways that Zionist Jewish communities across this continent actively and explicitly attempt to recruit any Jewish person (even the queer ones) to support or actively participate in the Israeli occupation. I am talking about softer invitations, the small print at the bottom of our social contracts which we are encouraged to minimize or zoom past as our hands are guided towards the dotted line.

Queers have been pushed to the margins and cast out of Jewish communities for generations, and many modern Jewish institutions and religious streams have doubled down on this exclusion. However, today we are seeing what appears to be a growing acceptance of queer peoples in certain Jewish spaces, and their increased inclusion in broader Jewish communities. This might compel you to think that queer Jews should be grateful, and should celebrate gaining a foothold in mainstream Jewish life. Sadly, I believe Groucho Marx got it right when he said, "I don't want to belong to any club that would accept me as one of its members". This might seem self-loathing or even downright

---

3 "Us" being anti-Zionist Jews both in diaspora and in occupied Palestinian territories.

ridiculous, but it holds a painful truth: Jewish queers have become politically desirable gamepieces in Zionism's long-term strategy against Palestinians and the Arab world at large. The synagogue with the Pride flag out front is still collecting money to fund Israeli missiles at the pulpit. The Queer Seder has an orange on the plate but no watermelon[4]. You can discuss the presence of queerness in Jewish faith and texts, but not the parts which forbid us from ever constructing a nation-state [4]. *This* is the violence we are invited to take part in: the implicit affirmation of these values that we provide by our mere presence in these spaces and communities.

The siloing of "LGBT inclusion" in Jewish spaces away from solidarity with other marginalized experiences has paved the path for greater participation in the Zionist project by those of us who had been so vehemently denied that same participation not so long ago. Queer Jews may not be monolithic, but I would nonetheless name a deep hunger for community as something we experience almost universally. Decades of rejection (and its ravages on bodies, minds, souls, relationships, and communities) have made us famished for inclusion. Now at long last we have been invited to the table, and we failed to see it was because they don't want us in the kitchen. We have lost sight of the cycles of history: we know that the pig may eat scraps from the Master's table, but it will wind up on the Master's plate nonetheless. Queer assimilation into fascism is nothing new[5] and has remained steadfast for decades all the way to the present day [5]. The barrier that is preventing queer Jews in the Australian colony from seeing their participation in this trend is the Zionist narrative of Jewish and Israeli exceptionalism, which produces a particularly enchanting brew when mixed with experiences of queer marginalization. Drunk on a blend of desperation, confusion, and isolation, with a few vigorous dashes of lifelong exposure to Zionist propaganda, many of us find ourselves stumbling around in the dark schism between "our" community and our righteousness. Suffice to say, I pray that recent events will sober up those of us who still think our "inclusion" is more meaningful than standing united against colonization, oligarchy, fascism, and mass death.

By now you might have noticed that I've successfully avoided providing any substantial summary of this book in this, my concluding chapter. Maybe this is a manifestation of my difficulty in parting with the manuscript, of bidding it farewell as it travels away from my grasp and towards the broader world. But I also believe that everything I have written throughout this book meets

---

4 A well-recognized symbol of Palestinian resistance.
5 Particularly for gay men.

at the very spearhead that is this chapter. We cannot gain any meaningful understanding of the lived experiences of queer Jews, here or anywhere, without first developing an understanding of our unique and at times troubling position in contemporary politics. I cannot discuss queer Jewish oppression and multi-point marginalization without naming the ever-growing amorphous blob of queer assimilationism that is co-opting vulnerable people and their most fragile aspects to create dazzle camouflage for a war machine. We cannot understand queer and/or Jewish insularity without seeing the ways our communities have isolated themselves from their Palestinian siblings both in occupied Palestine and in the Australian colony. All the queer theory in the world isn't worth the dust on my shoe if we can't use it to navigate contradictions and paradoxes on our way to total liberation.

So rather than tie this book in a bow, I instead offer a rope. It begins in my palm and extends across the ground, snaking towards the horizon into an imperceptible void. At the other end is a future we dream of, one of abundance, of deep connections to ourselves, each other, and the lands we are living on. It is a future that might get closer if we just grasp this rope in our hands and *pull*. This book is an invitation: you, me, and everyone else, shoulder to shoulder, dragging a glistening and beautiful world out of the darkest well.

References

[1] Ritchie J. Pinkwashing, homonationalism, and Israel–Palestine: The conceits of queer theory and the politics of the ordinary. *Antipode* 2015; 47: 616–634.

[2] Jeffers SJ. *Feel the Fear and Do It Anyway*. Ballantine, 1988.

[3] The Associated Press. NYC protesters demand Israeli cease-fire, at least 200 detained after filling Grand Central station. *AP News*, <https://apnews.com/article/gaza-israel-hamas-protest-grand-central-nypd-b6ceeb689b3d3c1e02a9a57f4796c048> (2023, accessed 30 October 2023).

[4] Salmon Y. Zionism and anti-Zionism in traditional Judaism in Eastern Europe. In: Reinharz J, Shapira A (eds). *Zionism and Religion*. UPNE, 1998.

[5] Osoy D. Flirting with Supremacy: Gay Men and the White Nationalist Movement.

AFTERWORD: ZIPPORAH, QUEEN
OF THE DESERT

When I first came up with the title for this book, I thought I was just being a little bit clever. Why not take the title of an iconic queer Australian film (Priscilla, Queen of the Desert) and amalgamate it with an iconic woman in the Torah (Zipporah)? It was a good pun, and it beat several other contenders with much less impact. However, as I have progressed through this project, and immersed myself more in both the core and the borderlands of the research topic, I've come to realize just how meaningful this choice of title has become. Zipporah was the first wife of Moses, a Midianite who was wedded to him by her father and who subsequently converts to Judaism. Her story is one of the more detailed and prominent tales to discuss circumcision [1], not only as a process but as a means of defence from a Divine attack [2]. By circumcising Jacob, one of Moses' children, she prevents an Angel from bringing harm onto the family, though the details as to the reason for the attack *or* why this spontaneous circumcision prevents further harm remain shrouded in mystery [3]. Zipporah is soon after rewarded by Moses with abandonment prior to Exodus, and he later remarries and has little contact with her [4].

There are so many themes swirling around this singular anecdote, a tiny story in the much larger narrative of Moses as the saviour of the Jewish people. Analysis of this story could easily be turned into its own book: there is betrayal, conversion, love, boundary-crossing, blood... This narrative has it all. When it comes to this story's relevance to this book, there are several notable themes that I felt compelled to highlight. Firstly, it is impossible to deny that a supposed "outsider" to Judaism, someone who married into the faith rather than be born into it, enacted a sacred rite in such a powerful way that even a Divine Being veered away from her path. This is such a rich description of the ways Judaism and Jewish people have always thrived from mingling with people outside of our culture and faith. Not only do we try to be a light unto others, but others are often the reason we are spared agony, suffering, and loss. To be clear, I am not suggesting that Zipporah was outside of Judaism; however, the narrative is such that she comes from "outside" and to "outside" she returns, her story ending with her going back to her father's home after Moses rejects her.

This rejection is also important to consider: why was Zipporah considered so expendable, despite her contributions? What was it about Moses' asceticism and Jewish puritanism that prevented Zipporah from being accepted into the community? No doubt her Black skin and her being born a gentile played a significant role. Here too we see equivalences with the experiences discussed throughout this book. Queer and trans people, especially those who are also "outside" of normative Jewish life in other ways (e.g. coming from interfaith marriages, being People of Colour), are often more likely to exist at the margins of Jewish societies and communities. Our contributions are never enough to save us from potential rejection and ostracization, and many Rabbinic laws have been established which can be used to intentionally exclude us.

There is also something visceral and resonant about the circumcision itself: a bold and intense act upon a body that saves a life. Circumcision's interconnectivity with transness here is particularly pertinent, especially in light of more recent halakhic considerations around the necessity of circumcision for transgender women [5]. Indeed, circumcision is an affirmation of gender in Jewish law, and here in this little footnote of a story we see a gender-affirming intervention that carries immense spiritual force. Zipporah provides Jacob with something that even his father did not bother to take care of and saves Moses' son from further harm in doing so. There is much to be said here about Divine bloodshed, about reimagining bodily interventions which one might view as acts of mutilation, about understanding that the body is not a neutral object to be kept pristine but a field of play (and battle) between ourselves, each other, and the Divine.

Finally, I have to highlight that although Priscilla went through the desert and found her place, Zipporah was never given the opportunity to be a part of the Exodus. She was left behind, despite keeping arguably the most powerful prophet in Jewish mythology alive. She never crossed the desert, never got to be in the Promised Land, never got to both suffer and thrive with the people to whom she rightfully belonged. At the end of the day, Zipporah was a Jew who was kept away from her community by a patriarch who did not see fit to include her in his plan for Jewish liberation. In a way, I'm hoping this book can provide Zipporah with a posthumous travel through these important deserts: the desert on the way to the Holy Land, the deserts of this beautiful continent that we call "Australia", the deserts that we have all crossed in our paths to finding peace within ourselves. If Priscilla could do it with a little help along the way, then we too can see the Zipporah in ourselves and in others and make sure she too can find a land of milk and honey to delight in.

References

[1] Glick NS. Zipporah and the Bridegroom of Blood: Searching for the Antecedents of Jewish Circumcision. In: Denniston GC, Gallo PG, Hodges FM, et al. (eds). *Bodily Integrity and the Politics of Circumcision: Culture, Controversy, and Change.* Dordrecht: Springer Netherlands, pp. 37–47.

[2] Blumenthal F. The circumcision performed by Zipporah. *Jewish Bible Quarterly* 2007; 35: 255–260.

[3] Robinson BP. Zipporah to the rescue: A contextual study of Exodus Iv 24–6. *Vetus Testamentum* 1986; 36: 447–473.

[4] Meyers C, Craven T, Kraemer RS. *Women in Scripture: A Dictionary of Named and Unnamed Women in the Hebrew Bible, the Apocryphal/Deuterocanonical Books and the New Testament.* HMH, 2000.

[5] Irshai R. The construction of gender in halakhic Responsa by the Reform movement: transgender people as a case study. *Journal of Modern Jewish Studies* 2019; 18: 160–176.

INDEX

COUNTERPOINTS

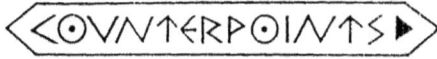

Studies in Criticality

Series Editor
Shirley R. Steinberg

Counterpoints publishes the most compelling and imaginative books being written in Education and Cultural Studies today. Grounded on the theoretical advances in critical theory, feminism, and postcolonialism in the last two decades of the twentieth century, Counterpoints engages the meaning of these innovations in various forms of educational expression. Committed to the proposition that theoretical literature should be accessible to a variety of audiences, the series insists that its authors avoid esoteric and jargonistic languages that transform educational scholarship into an elite discourse for the initiated. Scholarly work matters only to the degree it affects consciousness and practice at multiple sites. The editorial policy of *Counterpoints* is based on these principles and the ability of scholars to break new ground, to open new conversations, to go where educators have never gone before.

For additional information about this series or for the submission of manuscripts, please contact:

Shirley R. Steinberg, Series Editor
msgramsci@gmail.com

To order other books in this series, please contact our Customer Service Department:

peterlang@presswarehouse.com (within the U.S.)
orders@peterlang.com (outside the U.S.)

Or browse online by series:

www.peterlang.com

www.ingramcontent.com/pod-product-compliance
Lightning Source LLC
Chambersburg PA
CBHW071414290326
41932CB00047B/2956